"Anxiety can be a prison that prevents us from living and loving fully. In this beautifully organized workbook, we are guided through a powerful set of mindfulness tools and teachings that have the power to open the prison door. I'd recommend this to anyone struggling with anxiety or simply seeking a deeper taste of the healing potential of mindfulness."

—**Tara Brach, PhD**, author of *Radical Acceptance* and *True Refuge*

"Mindfulness is the way through the jingle jangle morning we keep waking to. Socrates said, 'Know thyself.' This is how."

—**Stephen Levine**, author of *Who Dies?*, *Meetings at the Edge*, and *A Year to Live*

"Anxiety clouds the mind. Mindfulness can foster the ability to see things as they are. Anxiety is painful. Mindfulness can be a pathway to mental and bodily ease. By bringing together the ailment and the cure, this book fills a real need. By doing so with care and skill, Bob, Florence, and Lynn provide the most needed nourishment."

—**Gregory Kramer, PhD**, guiding teacher at Metta Foundation and author of *Insight Dialogue*

"Whether you struggle with anxiety and panic, or simply wish to navigate the stresses of daily life with more peacefulness and balance, *A Mindfulness-Based Stress Reduction Workbook for Anxiety* offers trustworthy guidance and companionship on your journey toward wholeness. By cultivating mindfulness in this present moment, we discover liberation from the shackles of worry and anxiety that prevent us from living our love and giving the gifts we have come here to give."

—**John Robbins**, author of *Diet for a New America*, *The Food Revolution*, *Healthy at 100*, *The New Good Life*, and *Reclaiming Our Health*

"This masterful workbook integrates the rigor of science, the wisdom of reflection, and the effectiveness of years of clinical experience. The wealth of the ideas and practices presented in this educational, practical, and experiential workbook will be of benefit to anyone living with fear and anxiety, as well as to therapists and educators. Grounded in mindfulness, this workbook offers a new way of living that has the power to transform our individual and collective lives."

—**Shauna Shapiro, PhD**, coauthor of *Mindful Discipline*

"Who among us has not suffered from anxiety at one point or another? This skillfully-crafted, wise, and compassionate book offers a thorough and much-needed mindfulness approach to dealing with anxiety. The practical exercises, real-life stories, and heartfelt encouragement will benefit anyone who undertakes the journey to alleviate and transform anxiety."

—**Diana Winston**, director of Mindfulness Education at UCLA's Mindful Awareness Research Center and coauthor of *Fully Present: The Science, Art, and Practice of Mindfulness*

"Mindfulness-based stress reduction (MBSR) is currently the gold standard of mindfulness training, and this workbook [features] the essentials of MBSR written entirely for the anxious person. It's like having the finest MBSR teachers speaking personally with you and guiding you on the path to emotional freedom. The course material is presented in a gentle, easy-to-read, carefully sequenced manner. If you follow along closely—using the downloadable guided meditations for support—your life will surely change for the better. I highly recommend this book for anyone who struggles with anxiety."

—**Christopher Germer, PhD**, clinical instructor at Harvard Medical School, author of *The Mindful Path to Self-Compassion*, and coeditor of *Mindfulness and Psychotherapy*

A Mindfulness-Based Stress Reduction Workbook for Anxiety

BOB STAHL, PhD
FLORENCE MELEO-MEYER, MS, MA
LYNN KOERBEL, MPH

New Harbinger Publications, Inc.

Publisher's Note

This publication is designed to provide accurate and authoritative information in regard to the subject matter covered. It is sold with the understanding that the publisher is not engaged in rendering psychological, financial, legal, or other professional services. If expert assistance or counseling is needed, the services of a competent professional should be sought.

Distributed in Canada by Raincoast Books

New Harbinger Publications, Inc.
5674 Shattuck Avenue
Oakland, CA 94609
www.newharbinger.com

Cover design by Amy Shoup; Edited by Jasmine Star; Acquired by Jess O'Brien

Library of Congress Cataloging-in-Publication Data

Stahl, Bob.
A mindfulness-based stress reduction workbook for anxiety / Bob Stahl, PhD, Florence Meleo-Meyer, MS, MA, and Lynn Koerbel, MPH ; foreword by Saki Santorelli, EdD, MA.
pages cm
Includes bibliographical references.
ISBN 978-1-60882-973-6 (paperback) -- ISBN 978-1-60882-974-3 (pdf e-book) -- ISBN 978-1-60882-975-0 (epub)
1. Anxiety--Treatment. 2. Stress management. 3. Stress (Psychology) 4. Mind and body. 5. Mediation therapy. I. Meleo-Meyer, Florence. II. Koerbel, Lynn. III. Title.
RC531.S68 2014
616.85'22--dc23

2014025227

Printed in the United States of America

18 17 16

10 9 8 7 6 5 4 3 2

To those living with anxiety who looked within and discovered deeper wisdom and compassion.

Contents

	Acknowledgments	vii
	Foreword	ix
	Introduction	1
1	What Is Anxiety?	11
2	What Is Mindfulness?	27
3	Mindfulness and Anxiety	45
4	A Mindful Way of Meeting Anxiety in the Body	57
5	A Mindful Way of Meeting Anxious Thoughts	79
6	A Mindful Way of Meeting Anxious Emotions	101
7	Mindful Communication	115
8	Transforming Anxiety with Reconciliation and Loving-Kindness	129
9	MBSR Tools for Day-to-Day Living	143
10	Continuing the Journey	155
	Resources	167
	References	171

Acknowledgments

I want to deeply acknowledge my beloved wife, Jan, and our two sons, Ben and Bodhi. They continue to teach me so much about kindness, forgiveness, love, and support. Thanks also to my dear parents, Marilyn and Alvan, who embody life to the fullest with unending and endearing love. Salutations and bows to my meditation teachers: Rina Sircar, Taungpulu Sayadaw, Hlaing Tet Sayadaw, and Pakokku Sayadaw; I would not be on this mindful path without them. Deep gratitude to my dear friends Jon Kabat-Zinn, for birthing MBSR, and to Saki Santorelli, executive director at the Center for Mindfulness at the University of Massachusetts Medical School; both bring mindfulness so skillfully into the world, along with the science to support it, to the great benefit of so many. I also want to thank my dear dhamma sisters Florence Meleo-Meyer and Lynn Koerbel, who partnered with me in writing this book. They are an embodiment of wisdom, integrity, and heart. Lastly, deep gratitude for all of my friends and students, and for all beings great and small who teach me humility and compassion.

—Bob

Participating in this unfolding mystery and beauty of life is like a fountain of love beyond words. I would like to lovingly acknowledge my children and their partners: Anna and Seth, Nick and Alexis, and Luke and India, and my grandchildren, Odette and Eden.

With gratitude, I honor my teachers: Swami Chidvilasananda, whose abundant grace continues to awaken the light of wholeness in every moment; Jon Kabat-Zinn and Saki Santorelli, whose dedication, brilliance, and generosity have paved the way for me and thousands more to savor the preciousness of life; and Gregory Kramer, whose teaching embodies remembrance of oneness, stillness, and silence. I want to thank my circle of family, friends, and colleagues. You embody kindness and companionship as our life together deepens. Bob Stahl and Lynn Koerbel, I treasure your presence. Sharing kindred heart, vision, and effort with this book has been an offering of love.

—Florence

I offer gratitude to my teachers, especially Swami Chidvilasananda, who first showed me that the beauty and light in each heart is accessible and knowable. A bow to my partner in life and love, Annie Bissett, whose constancy, deep heart, and clear-eyed seeing has held me steady through all kinds of inner and outer weather, knowing when to urge me forward—and when to offer refuge. And to my parents, Wally and Shirley Koerbel. They taught me first, and I return over and over to their early lessons of hard work, caring for others, and leading with love. To Jon Kabat-Zinn, whose clear vision and fine offering have touched so many through the gift of MBSR, and to Saki Santorelli, who leads with energy and a heart on fire. Finally, but not least, to my dear, sweet writing and dhamma friends, Bob Stahl and Florence Meleo-Meyer. Their commitment to the relief of suffering is inspiring, and I am honored to know them.

—Lynn

We thank Saki Santorelli, PhD, who so lovingly supported our project and graciously wrote the foreword. We also want to express our deep thanks to others who blessed our book: Tara Brach, Stephen Levine, Diana Winston, Gregory Kramer, John Robbins, Shauna Shapiro, and Christopher Germer. We extend appreciation to our friends who modeled for the yoga illustrations: Heidi Haas-Hooven, Fred Hooven, Jodie Nolan, and Jonathan Thomas. In addition, we feel deep gratitude to the team at New Harbinger who stewarded this book and guided us in making it the best it could be: Jess O'Brien, Nicola Skidmore, Jess Beebe, and freelance copy editor extraordinaire Jasmine Star.

—Bob, Florence, and Lynn

Foreword

Some time ago, on a Thursday morning, I was sitting in a circle with thirty people participating in the Stress Reduction Clinic at the University of Massachusetts Medical School. Our clinic is the place of origin of mindfulness-based stress reduction. MBSR was developed thirty-five years ago by my longtime friend and colleague Jon Kabat-Zinn, and it has been continually taught and researched at UMass since 1979. More than twenty thousand people have completed our program at UMass, and scientific research about mindfulness and MBSR has grown exponentially and globally during the last ten years.

Who were the participants in that circle? I could tell you about John, the surgeon, who six months earlier underwent open-heart surgery to repair a defective valve; or about Dorothy, a high-school teacher with persistent angina, who said she is always nice, never asserts herself, and feels "squeezed" most of the time. However, since the central theme of this book is anxiety and the ways we can learn to integrate mindfulness into our lives as a means of loosing the bonds that imprison and impoverish us when we are in the grip of unproductive anxiety, I'm going to tell you about Marie.

Marie sat right next to the door, wearing dark sunglasses. Her cheeks glistened with tears. She told us she had been a high-powered businesswoman for a long time and that she was used to being accomplished and in control, functioning as everyone's caretaker. Now, she told us, she felt severe and almost constant anxiety accompanied by episodes of terror. Someone had had to drive her to class that morning; Marie was filled with fear. She went everywhere with a big bag, a kind of survival kit containing water bottles, keys, address books, an array of medicine, inspirational readings, and other items. The bag was on the floor, tucked close to her. She told us about this bag—half laughing, half crying—as a way of describing her predicament. She said she wanted to "be like I used to be" but was plagued with thoughts about the future: *What will happen to me? What if this or that happens? How long can I go on like this? What if I don't get better?* I was struck most powerfully by her final testament: "I want to take back my life."

Like Marie, don't we all want to inhabit this one life we have to live as fully as possible?

Mindfulness and MBSR are not panaceas. There is, however, mounting scientific evidence of their effectiveness for a wide range of conditions. For example, in March 2014, after reviewing in detail nearly nineteen thousand meditation studies and sorting through forty-seven well-designed clinical trials, researchers from Johns Hopkins University published an article in the *Journal of the American Medical Association Internal Medicine* reporting that meditation and particularly mindfulness meditation can help ease anxiety, depression, and pain (Goyal et al. 2014). This is very good news!

What are tens of thousands of MBSR participants all over the world learning? In order to dispel stereotypical notions about meditation and mindfulness, let's begin with what they are *not* learning: They are not learning to withdraw and "go someplace else." They are not learning to simply relax, or zone out, or empty their minds, or visualize themselves in a special, safe place, or deny that they have anxiety.

Instead, they are learning something both simpler and more profound: how to be become attentive to the moment-to-moment actuality of their lives—body and mind, heart and soul. Through this attending to the actuality of being alive, they are learning to cultivate greater awareness. Through this awareness, they are learning how to stop, to step back just enough to begin to realize directly and unambiguously how totally immersed in and identified with thinking they are—particularly those worrisome and anxiety-provoking thoughts that easily carry them away. This stepping back is a lot like waking up from a terrifying dream. And in this waking up, they are becoming increasingly capable of *turning toward* the very sensations and thoughts that have up until now generated unbridled worry, fear, and anxiety.

Something is changing through this radical act of awareness. Program participants become increasingly familiar with what it feels like to be present. They begin moving from being conditioned, highly reactive, and enmeshed in anxiety-provoking mind states to becoming awake, responsive, and more capable of making life-enhancing choices. They are discovering that they have options—new ways of responding to familiar situations and circumstances. And while this turning toward what they would rather avoid seems counterintuitive, people consistently report that the MBSR practice of learning to see and meet directly what's on their minds and in their bodies unmasks the habits that have driven them to believe that these thoughts are "theirs," that they are "real," and that they are "true" and always will be. This is revelatory. Through the MBSR program, participants are learning more about themselves, *unlearning* a host of old habits of mind that are no longer helpful, and discovering that they can face into feelings of anxiety in ways that are liberating.

I suspect we all want this same kind of freedom.

This is what Marie meant about taking back her life. In the early weeks of the course, Marie took off her sunglasses. Halfway through the program, she began to drive. One day she laughed out loud about that "big bag" she no longer carried. Did she still feel highly anxious at times? Yes. But she no longer felt helpless in the face of anxiety, and more importantly the thoughts and feelings that used to generate fear and the sense of isolation no longer dominated her life. In a very real way, Marie was liberating herself through the direct experience of learning mindfulness.

This book is a key that you are now holding in your hand. It fits the lock and opens the door to the prison of anxiety and fear. Then it gently and persistently escorts you out into the freshness that you are and that awaits you every day of your life.

Written by three renowned MBSR teachers and expert guides, Bob Stahl, Florence Meleo-Meyer, and Lynn Koerbel, the text is clear, kind, and unremitting in its message that anxiety is workable. The authors are masters at helping you understand just how vast this word "workable" really is. I love the term "workable." It is hopeful, and implies that you are now entering into a *relationship* with anxiety and have within you all the requisite resources to free yourself from the narrow confines that anxiety can construct.

If you suffer from anxiety and want to live with greater ease, contentment, and understanding, this book is for you. If you want to discover just how big and bright and beautiful you already are, this book is a map leading you into the treasure that is you.

—Saki F. Santorelli, EdD, MA
Professor of Medicine
Director, Stress Reduction Clinic
Executive Director, Center for Mindfulness in Medicine, Health Care, and Society
University of Massachusetts Medical School

Introduction

Welcome to *A Mindfulness-Based Stress Reduction Workbook for Anxiety*. If you're living with anxiety, you are not alone. In 2008, the National Institute of Mental Health reported that approximately forty million American adults suffer from anxiety disorders. The costs of this epidemic of anxiety are staggering, including in economic terms, with one study finding that anxiety disorders cost the United States more than $42 billion a year, almost one-third of the country's $148 billion total mental health bill (Greenberg et al. 1999).

Anxiety differs from normal feelings of nervousness. People living with anxiety are more prone to depression and dependence on or abuse of alcohol and other substances to seek relief from their symptoms. Anxiety can be paralyzing, affecting many spheres of life, from home and social life to the workplace.

Causes and Types of Anxiety

Chapter 1 is devoted to a discussion of anxiety, so we'll just touch on a few basic points here. The causes of anxiety disorders are not fully understood. In most cases, anxiety isn't caused by a single factor, instead developing from a complex set of risk factors that includes brain chemistry, genetics, personality, life events, and environmental stresses. Sometimes physical factors can contribute, ramping up feelings of anxiety in the body and mind. Common culprits include caffeine consumption, a very active thyroid (hyperthyroidism), low blood sugar (hypoglycemia), heart arrhythmia, or eating a lot of sugary foods with few complex carbs to help control blood sugar. In addition, some medications and herbs may have side effects that increase susceptibility to anxiety. Therefore, it may be helpful to consult with a health professional to rule out or address physical causes. All of that said, it's also fair to say that most anxiety is rooted in the psyche. This book is dedicated to exploring how a mindfulness-based intervention can lessen your anxiety and improve your well-being.

There are many types of anxiety disorders, including panic disorder, social anxiety disorder, posttraumatic stress disorder, obsessive-compulsive disorder, generalized anxiety disorder, agoraphobia, and specific phobias, such as fear of flying, spiders, and so on. In this book, we mostly focus on generalized and social anxiety, since these are the most common forms of anxiety. However, as you practice mindfulness, you'll see its relevance to other forms of anxiety.

Anxiety symptoms can vary depending on the type of anxiety, but they often include feelings of panic, fear, apprehension, and uneasiness. Anxiety is often associated with worries about the future and perceived threats. You may have thoughts like *I'm really feeling anxious about going to the work picnic. When I'm nervous, I don't feel at ease with myself. How am I going to handle this?* When you have these types of thoughts and the emotions associated with them, you're likely to feel them in your body, perhaps having an upset stomach or muscle tension. Other physical effects include insomnia, headaches, cold or sweaty hands or feet, heart palpitations, shortness of breath, dry mouth, numbness or tingling in the hands, and rashes or other skin problems. Alternatively, or in addition, the feelings may express themselves as a physical behavior, like biting your nails, overeating, or undereating.

Anxiety can have a significant impact on family relationships. It can also be detrimental to day-to-day activities, extending to job performance and work effectiveness, as it often results in a diminished ability to concentrate. You may experience obsessive thoughts, sleep disturbances, or an inability to be calm and still. Anxiety can also exacerbate the stress of living with an illness, since it increases the overall burden of suffering and distress.

Whereas fear is most often directed toward a specific external event, situation, or object, anxiety is a more internal, vague worry about something bad happening. We want to acknowledge that experiencing fear from time to time is normal. As a matter of fact, human beings and other animals are wired to feel fear; it's part of our biological survival system and arises in the amygdala, a primitive brain structure that senses threats and triggers the fight-or-flight reaction. In appropriate situations, this response helps us move and act with speed and clarity. The distinction between normal fear and anxiety begins to blur when the perceived threat isn't something that literally puts you at physical risk but instead represents a psychological or emotional threat. These experiences tend to have no real end and therefore can take over, preoccupying your mind and limiting your life.

About the Authors

We'd like to tell you a bit about ourselves and why we wrote this book. Each of us has been affected by anxiety and feels blessed to have been introduced to mindfulness practice. For all three of us, mindfulness has been transformative, not only helping us meet moments of anxiety, but also allowing us to discover other inner resources, such as courage, resiliency, humor, and insight. We want to affirm that it's possible to live with less anxiety and experience more ease within your being, and to that end we offer this book, from our hearts to yours.

Bob Stahl

I am quite familiar with the rush of anxiety and how it can stream through my skin, flesh, bones, and being. It has ranged from feeling slightly anxious in social situations to worries about the future or my loved ones. I also experienced major anxiety when I had a life-threatening illness in 1996, nearly dying from necrotizing fasciitis, more popularly known as flesh-eating bacteria. I was immensely grateful for my practice of mindfulness meditation, which helped me get through that extreme health crisis.

Over the years, my mindfulness practice has been a constant source of refuge, especially during times of anxiety, whether marginal or severe anxiety. Since my first mindfulness meditation retreat many years ago, I've learned to use this practice as a way to turn into my fears and find my heart. As my beloved meditation teacher Rina Sircar would say, "Acknowledgment will bring you knowledge." And sure enough, when I began to acknowledge my anxiety, in time it gradually dissipated. I've discovered that the way around anxiety is to turn into it, just like turning the wheels of a car into a skid to get back on track. Mindfulness practice has truly transformed my life, and I'm happy to offer this book to you so you can experience similar benefits.

Florence Meleo-Meyer

When I was sixteen, I struggled with a series of panic attacks following a crisis in my family. During those episodes, I felt shortness of breath and other physical sensations, such as shakiness and tightness in my head, chest, and stomach. I felt a sense of confused helplessness and feared losing control. I didn't know what these episodes were, or even that they could be associated with the family stress I was experiencing. Perhaps because of that early suffering, I began to be interested in what it meant to be human, and this led me to the practice of meditation.

Through practicing mindfulness, I began to turn toward what I experienced because it was right there, in the moment. Whether I was experiencing judgment, shakiness, or fear of some inadequacy, the power of embracing my own experience with a degree of kindness and gentleness allowed my body to settle, my mind to ease, and my heart to expand with compassion toward myself. I am grateful beyond words for the gift of mindfulness meditation and the possibility to open to being fully alive, with the entire mix of experiences, emotions, challenges, and gifts life brings. Living mindfully allows me to embrace my life through times of both sunshine and shadow. Mindfulness practice offers me a path toward freedom from my suffering, and this is worth sharing! May you touch freedom from anxiety through this book, chapter by chapter, as you learn and practice mindfulness.

Lynn Koerbel

I was the kid who couldn't do sleepovers or go away to camp because being away from home felt overwhelming. I was also often anxious at school. A queasy stomach and physical symptoms I didn't understand sent me home sick many times. Now, upon reflection, I see that they were telltale signs of anxiety. As I got older, my experience of anxiety continued to limit my activities. One small example is that I made the difficult decision to not participate in piano recitals because I couldn't face the added pressure of memorization.

Two important behaviors helped shift this for me. One was vigorous aerobic activity; the other was meditation and yoga, which I discovered in high school. Consciously moving my body and focusing my awareness opened more choices to me in the moment and offered a measure of self-control, fortitude, and emotional freedom. Over the years, my steadfast practice of mindfulness has transformed the experience of anxiety from a looming monster into a familiar teacher—one who offers me the opportunity to look deeper at what's actually happening, to acknowledge all of my feelings, and to step beyond my comfort zone into what my heart is calling out for. In addition to my own experience, I've also had the honor to sit with clients and students who have courageously turned toward their anxiety—the very thing that is most distressing—finding both refuge and transformation through mindfulness practice.

Who This Workbook Is For

This educational, practical, and experiential workbook is for anyone living with fear and anxiety, whether related to the vicissitudes of daily life, illness or physical pain, or other factors. It will guide you in developing a mindfulness practice that will not only help you reduce anxiety but also steer you toward a life of greater ease, vitality, and well-being. In addition, this workbook may be useful for therapists, clinicians, or educators as an adjunct in working with anxious clients or students.

The approach in this book was inspired by the pioneering work of Jon Kabat-Zinn, PhD, who founded the mindfulness-based stress reduction (MBSR) program, and Saki Santorelli, EdD, director of the Center for Mindfulness at the University of Massachusetts Medical School. While this workbook isn't a replacement for taking an MBSR course, we do believe it can be very helpful in alleviating anxiety. (To find an MBSR program in your area, see the Resources section at the back of the book.)

Mindfulness has become a hot item, making huge inroads in the worlds of medicine, neuroscience, psychology, education, and business. Mindfulness-based interventions are spreading across the world and helping many people who live with stress, pain, illness, depression, addiction, and, of course, anxiety.

Overview of the Book

This workbook is a practical guide that will introduce you to mindfulness as a way of life. Mindfulness can be experienced in two ways: through informal and formal practices. With informal practice, you bring mindfulness into your everyday life, being mindful as you wash the dishes, sweep the floor, brush your teeth, and so on. You can practice informally while eating, having a conversation with someone, or working—whatever you may be doing. Formal practice is more structured and includes various guided meditations that we'll introduce in this book, such as mindful breathing, the body scan, sitting meditation, and loving-kindness meditation. For these practices, you can either read them in the book or listen to the audio versions available for download at http://www.newharbinger.com/29736. (See the back of this book for information on how to access the downloadable content.)

We also include important information on the mind-body connection and the science of mindfulness that will deepen your understanding of anxiety and help you learn to manage it better, along with exercises to increase your resilience and sense of ease in life. Here's a brief overview of the chapters, followed by a description of some of the special elements you'll encounter throughout the book.

Chapter 1: What Is Anxiety? In chapter 1, we explore anxiety, its biological roots, and how it relates to stress.

Chapter 2: What Is Mindfulness? In chapter 2, we introduce mindfulness and mindfulness-based stress reduction (MBSR). We discuss attitudes that are important in developing a mindfulness practice, including befriending yourself as you are, even while living with anxiety. We also address challenges that may arise during meditation and how to work with them.

Chapter 3: Mindfulness and Anxiety. In chapter 3, we discuss how mindfulness can help with anxiety and address the difference between reacting and responding. Mindlessly reacting to anxiety often produces more distress and is therefore counterproductive. Responding mindfully, on the other hand, is a much more constructive way of dealing with anxiety.

Chapter 4: A Mindful Way of Meeting Anxiety in the Body. In chapter 4, we focus on practices for working with anxiety in the body. Although you might think it's counterintuitive to mindfully turn toward anxious feelings in the body, it's actually a helpful way to begin to acclimate yourself to those feelings and befriend your body as a messenger that can help alert you to your experience. In addition, tuning in to physical sensations, even those related to anxiety, is a powerful way to bring yourself into the here and now, since sensations exist only in the present moment.

Chapter 5: A Mindful Way of Meeting Anxious Thoughts. In chapter 5, we explore how certain thinking patterns can feed anxiety, especially excessive worries about the future and what-if thoughts. You'll learn practices that will help you not take your thoughts so seriously or personally, allowing you to experience that thoughts are just thoughts, not a complete definition of who you are. By bringing mindfulness to anxious thoughts, you can cultivate more peace within.

Chapter 6: A Mindful Way of Meeting Anxious Emotions. In chapter 6 we explore how anxiety affects emotions and how to work with anxiety-related feelings. Here too, it's helpful, if counterintuitive, to turn toward these challenging experiences, and we'll offer several practices that will help you do just that.

Chapter 7: Mindful Communication. The impact of what you say to others (and yourself) is huge. Communication can make you feel either safe and at ease or deeply distressed and racked with anxiety. In chapter 7, you'll learn to bring more mindfulness to communication.

Chapter 8: Transforming Anxiety with Reconciliation and Loving-Kindness. Just like a bird needs two wings to fly, mindfulness alone isn't enough for working with anxiety—or for living a full life. Compassion is also necessary. When you put them together and bring mindfulness to reconciliation and loving-kindness, the result is a synergy and wisdom that neither wing possesses on its own.

Chapter 9: MBSR Tools for Day-to-Day Living. In chapter 9, you'll learn to deepen your awareness of the present moment by using your senses and grounding in your body and breath as you go about your everyday life. We'll also guide you in exploring what you tend to take in (not just food and beverages but also exercise, sleep, the media, technology, and social contact) and how all of this affects you.

Chapter 10: Continuing the Journey. In the last chapter, we'll launch you fully into a life of greater freedom from anxiety, with a deeper sense of connection to yourself, others, the world, and even the universe.

Resources. At the end of the book, we provide information on organizations, books, and other resources that can help you maintain your mindfulness practice as a way of life. Inspirational and informative readings and spending time with like-minded people can really support your mindfulness practice.

How to Use This Workbook

We recommend that you work through this book slowly and sequentially, beginning with chapter 1, since it's organized to help you progressively develop your mindfulness practice. As you work your way through the book, please remember to be patient and compassionate with yourself. This is a gradual process, and it will take time, just like learning to play a musical instrument; but when you put sincere effort into it, you'll eventually be playing a beautiful melody. Practice is the key to true and lasting change, so take as long as you wish to work through each chapter before moving on to the next. This will help you integrate the practices into your life.

In addition to offering mindfulness practices and information on how to mindfully work with anxiety, each chapter also includes special elements to enhance your learning and help you stay on track:

- **Mindful Journaling:** We provide space for you to journal about your experiences when you do a practice for the first time. Feel free to keep a separate journal for this purpose if you like—or if you really get into it and would like more space. Capturing what you're learning and noticing, along with any insights along the way, can provide valuable documentation of your journey. Over time, this can remind you that you're making progress, even when you experience occasional setbacks.

- **Mindful Exploration:** These sections invite you to take some time to reflect upon and explore various topics.

- **Mindful Pause:** Pausing to mindfully acknowledge your experience can do wonders in helping you integrate new learning, so from time to time, we'll offer a text box with a gentle reminder to take a mindful pause before turning your attention to something new.

- **Try This:** In these text boxes, you'll find strategies that can help you get a feel for mindfulness by taking a new approach to something familiar.

- **Practice logs:** Taking a page from the saying "What we measure grows," we provide space for you to record how your practice has been going. You can use this information to guide you in making any needed adjustments.
- **Downloadable audio files:** This workbook includes a number of guided meditations, and as mentioned, you can download all of them at http://www.newharbinger.com/29736. Listening to these meditations is a wonderful way to build your practice, since it sets the pace and allows you to focus on the practice without having to refer back to the book. The audio versions are also very portable; you can listen to them almost anywhere on an electronic device. Many of the meditations have options for practicing for different lengths of time—typically fifteen, thirty, or forty-five minutes, to help you build your practice gradually.

Like everything in life, your mindfulness practice will be ever changing. If at some point you notice that you've been slacking off in your practice, don't be hard on yourself. The beauty of mindfulness is that this very realization returns you to mindfulness. The moment you realize you haven't been present, you're present once again!

Mindful Exploration: Why You've Chosen to Work with This Book

Here, we'd like to invite you to engage in your first mindful exploration. As you write—here and in all of the mindful explorations—there's no need to judge, analyze, or figure anything out. Simply write about whatever bodily sensations, thoughts, or emotions you feel as you reflect upon the question. We suggest you take your time with these explorations so they can deepen within you, and feel free to use a separate journal if you'd like more space.

What's going on in your life that led you to purchase this book?

____

____

____

What are you hoping for as a result of working with this book?

____

____

____

What are some positive things that you can say about yourself or that others may say about you?

____

____

____

Exercise: Assessing Your Anxiety Level

Before you turn to chapter 1, take a moment to assess your current level of anxiety. This isn't a formal assessment; rather, it's meant to give you a snapshot of your perception of how you're feeling. There are two steps to this process:

1. Using the form below, list up to ten situations that you currently feel anxious about. Feel free to list everyday experiences of anxiety or really zero in on specific things. The more explicit you are, the better you'll be able to tell whether your anxiety levels have changed later, when you repeat this assessment at the end of the book.

2. Rate how you feel about each situation on a scale of 1 to 10, with 1 being not very anxious and 10 being extremely anxious.

Here's an example: Fred felt a lot of anxiety when he had to enter social situations. Going to restaurants was particularly hard, so he listed that as one of his items. When he completed the first assessment, he rated his anxiety level in that situation at 8, which was quite high. As he followed the approach in this book, he noticed that his anxiety level gradually decreased, ultimately lowering to just 3. He could definitely feel a positive change, and filling out this assessment also allowed him to see that his situation was improving.

One important note: If you assign high ratings (8 to 10) to most of the items you list, it would probably be a good idea to seek support from a health care or mental health professional as an adjunct to your work with this book.

Rating	Situation
______	______________________________
______	______________________________
______	______________________________
______	______________________________
______	______________________________
______	______________________________
______	______________________________
______	______________________________
______	______________________________
______	______________________________

MINDFUL PAUSE

Take a moment to thank yourself for filling out this assessment and tuning in to your anxiety level. Consciously turning toward your anxiety in this way can be difficult. By doing this, and by choosing to work with this book, you're taking an active step in participating in your health and well-being. Although there will be ups and downs, as you practice mindfulness you'll gain more balance in the midst of anxiety.

Chapter 1

What Is Anxiety?

A few months ago Lynn received a phone call at the Center for Mindfulness from a young man named Mark. His voice was strong and resolute as he listed the various issues affecting his mental and emotional well-being. His understanding was quite mature, and as she listened she was struck by his self-awareness and sincerity. He told Lynn that he'd had several panic attacks—one so severe he thought he was having a heart attack—and went on to describe his anxiety symptoms in detail and with great clarity. He was being treated for general anxiety disorder by a well-regarded psychiatrist and had also done a great deal of research into options for treatment. As he continued, Lynn wondered how she could add anything, given how thoughtfully he'd already addressed his plight. Then he said, "I'm calling you to see if mindfulness can help me. I'll do anything possible to *never, ever* feel panic and anxiety again."

When Lynn heard this, she felt deep empathy for this man. The experience of anxiety is, in itself, overwhelming and anxiety provoking, and most people would like to eradicate the experience entirely. So Lynn carefully responded, "But that's the difficulty, Mark. There's no way anyone can guarantee it will never happen again. We never know what will happen from one moment to the next, even though we want to believe there's a way to orchestrate reality to make things more comfortable for ourselves. These efforts give us a sense that we know what's going to happen, even though we don't. All of us are always only in this moment. *Now* is the only place our life actually happens—whether we've got anxiety or not."

The silence at the other end of the line made Lynn wonder if Mark was still there. She thought that perhaps she'd scared him. Finally he spoke, and she could hear the relief in his voice. "Wow. No one's ever said that before. The doctors have all been working with my medication to make sure it doesn't happen again, and I thought I'd also be able to do something that would shut the door on this thing. Wow..." More silence followed, and finally Lynn gently asked Mark what he was feeling. He answered in a tone that was deeper and more resonant than before: "Relief, actually. Now that I don't have any hope of having it go away, it feels like maybe I could face it."

Lynn smiled as she replied, "Well, that could be a real option."

Anxiety and Mindfulness

Your own experience of anxiety may range from mild to overwhelming. It may be brought on sporadically by various work or relationship issues or other life experiences. Or it may be a chronic state. You may already have sought assistance from a physician, psychiatrist, or other mental health professional, and you may be taking medications to help manage symptoms. You may have been diagnosed with an anxiety disorder, such as generalized anxiety disorder (GAD) or social anxiety disorder (SAD). In general, these diagnoses are made when symptoms become excessive, when anxiety arises with little or no provocation, or when anxiety reactions seem exaggerated in relation to the situations that bring them on.

The approaches in this book primarily target GAD and SAD, since these anxiety disorders are the most prevalent. However, if you suffer from panic attacks, post-traumatic stress disorder (PTSD), specific phobias, or obsessive-compulsive disorder (OCD), this book will also be helpful for you. In fact, anyone who struggles with anxiety can reap benefits from mindfulness and the practices offered here, regardless of diagnosis. If you struggle with anxious thoughts, worry, fearful anticipation of the future, or a sense of dread, this book will be useful for you.

One important note: If you're taking medication for your anxiety, please don't stop taking it because you're working with this book. Decreasing or stopping medication should only be done under the care of your prescribing doctor. Mindfulness can be a powerful method of working with anxiety, and it blends well with other approaches, including medications, psychotherapy, and counseling. Talk with your health care providers about the best way to integrate all of your treatments to obtain the greatest benefit.

Cara's Story

When Cara returned to college at age thirty-eight, she was unprepared for some of the emotions that arose. The opportunity to finish her degree was life changing, and she hadn't thought it would actually happen. She was excited and expected it to be a joyful journey of discovery. But as she began to attend classes and write papers, she was surprised to experience a great deal of anxiety. She worried that she didn't understand assignments and often feared that she wasn't on top of the material, even when her fellow students were just discussing their own opinions. Over time, her sleep became disturbed and her stomach always felt tight. Still, she plodded on, and she found learning and her relationships with her classmates and professors deeply satisfying even as she struggled with anxiety. And although her anxiety was distressing, Cara was also curious about it. Eventually, she decided to enroll in a mindfulness-based stress reduction class.

Through the mindfulness practices she learned in the MBSR classes and her own reflections, Cara explored her paradoxical feelings and eventually brought to light some important experiences in her early childhood education. She remembered distressing experiences with several controlling teachers, concerns about grades, and a few episodes when she felt confused and unsure and didn't feel she had anyone to talk to about it or get reassurance from. These insights helped Cara see that she had unconsciously brought her past experiences of formal education into her present situation and then projected them into the future so that she expected confusion, shame, and failure.

Cara could see how her anxiety was part of an unconscious effort to protect herself from emotional pain and perhaps failure. This insight allowed her to bring a new level of gentleness and care to herself as she continued to attend classes. She started actively looking for moments when her learning experiences were positive, and began to bring informal mindfulness practices into her classroom experience in small and simple ways. This helped her acknowledge that learning and being in school necessarily entailed some elements that weren't always comfortable, like competition and grades, but that there were also resources she could draw on so she didn't have to go it alone. In addition, she recognized that she couldn't be good at everything, and this allowed her to further ease up on herself. This didn't mean she never again felt anxious about school, but she was able to work within herself and increase her capacity to accept the entire experience of being back at school.

Coming to Terms with Anxiety

Fear is, of course, a component of anxiety. When experienced in the moment, perhaps in response to a sudden scare, fear resolves fairly quickly. However, if you then become worried that the fearful experience will happen again, this taps into the future, fueling anxiety.

This is where mental distress comes in, and based on our own experience, we understand all too well how thoughts and worries about future events can set the mind spinning out of control, making it difficult or impossible to concentrate and focus in the present. Anxiety also has emotional and physical aspects illuminated by the roots of the word "anxiety": the Latin *anxietas*, which means "anguish" or "solicitude," capturing the feeling of heart wringing and contraction that can accompany anxiety. The other Latin root associated with "anxiety" is *angere*, meaning "to choke or squeeze" or, more figuratively, "to torment or cause distress." This conveys the physical experience of tightness, constriction, and gripping that anxiety can create in the body.

"Anxiety" has many synonyms, including "fear," "foreboding," "worry," "disquiet," "tension," "unease," "restlessness," "watchfulness," "distress," "concern," "nervousness," and the all-encompassing "suffering." These words paint a more complete picture of the experience of anxiety, encompassing its physical, emotional, and cognitive symptoms. Just reading this list may make you actively consider the difficulties, challenges, and concerns in your life.

Now, just as importantly, consider some antonyms for anxiety: "certainty," "serenity," "tranquility," "assurance," "calm," "contentment," "happiness," "peacefulness," "bravery," "composure," and "confidence." Simply by reading this list, you might actually feel some of these qualities within you as well. All of these words, both synonyms and antonyms, are quite compelling and speak to the universality of human experience. We've all had moments of peace and tranquility, times when we were free of worry and confident; and we can touch those states even in remembrance.

Biological and Evolutionary Roots of Anxiety

Anxiety is part of a highly sensitive, biologically efficient threat-detection system that evolved to help us survive and thrive. Understanding that this system is part of a survival mechanism can be so helpful in taking a different stance toward anxiety. Because the neurological and other physiological systems involved are quite complex, we've simplified the following discussion for ease of understanding, and we particularly highlight how anxiety is triggered, since this is a key point where you can mindfully intervene to diminish your experience of anxiety.

The central nervous system has two main branches: the sympathetic and parasympathetic. When you encounter danger, the sympathetic nervous system is like a gas pedal, activating the fight-or-flight reaction or, more accurately, the fight, flight, or freeze reaction. In contrast, the parasympathetic nervous system acts like the brakes, restoring calm and equilibrium after activation of the sympathetic nervous system. These systems have been well studied in both humans and animals to determine the exact ways in which brain chemistry and hormones influence various body systems.

Activation of the sympathetic nervous system is like an alert, sending a signal that a threat is present. For our distant ancestors, this could have included being chased by wild animals or facing threatening weather conditions. Once danger has been detected, the system responds automatically and involuntarily. To promote survival, the sympathetic nervous system releases a surge of hormones and chemicals, including the stress hormones adrenaline and cortisol. These substances arouse the major systems of the body, setting off a cascade of reactions that affect the nervous system, musculoskeletal system, cardiovascular system, and immune system. To facilitate fighting or fleeing, blood flow is shunted away from internal organs and toward muscles in the extremities. The heart beats faster and harder, and respiratory rate increases and becomes shallower. In addition, the eyes dilate to better take in information from the environment, and all of the senses become sharper and more focused. The muscles around the eyes and throughout the face tense, which aids in narrowing the focus of attention to scanning the environment for danger and taking in information useful for a return to safety and security.

Once the imminent danger passes, the body is restored to balance by the activity of the parasympathetic nervous system. In this phase, the surge of stress hormones stops, musculoskeletal tension is released, and the body efficiently moves back to a state where digestion, assimilation, and regenerative physiological functions can occur.

Here's an example from the animal kingdom: Imagine a herd of gazelles peacefully grazing on the savannah. Suddenly a cheetah rushes into the group, causing a fight, flight, or freeze reaction throughout the herd, which bolts into action and flees. But when the chase ends (whether successfully or unsuccessfully for the cheetah), the herd comes back together and returns to a state of ease: grazing, resting, digesting, and otherwise engaging in typical activities.

As this example shows, the automaticity of the system is part of its genius. If the gazelles, or we humans, had to take the time to consciously process a dangerous event, we could easily get caught up in indecision or a decision-making process that would waste precious time. If you step out into traffic as a bus comes around the corner and a quick jolt of adrenaline gets you back to the curb in record time, the value of this swift, unconscious process is clear. There's no denying how valuable the fight, flight, or freeze reaction is.

The Primitive Brain's Limitations

It's hypothesized that our ancestors experienced danger in relatively small doses: a sudden encounter with a wild animal, a violent weather event, and so on. These days, we're less vulnerable to such immediate and violent threats. Instead, most of the "threats" we experience are in the social or emotional realm: someone cuts us off in traffic; our boss ignores a carefully compiled report or, worse, comments only on a small flaw; our partner accuses us of being selfish; a good friend forgets a lunch date. In these situations, what's at stake isn't our existence, but rather our reputation, self-worth, or feelings of being loved and emotionally safe. We may be able to rationalize that these experiences aren't actually life threatening, but thanks to the primitive brain, the body responds with the same fight, flight, or freeze reaction. The resulting muscular tension, tight gut, rapid heartbeat, and other physical sensations can be confusing, adding to a sense that the situation is dire and priming the brain to be on alert for future situations that somehow resemble the current "emergency."

In addition, because the fight, flight, or freeze reaction is so immediate (again, a good thing when it comes to physical danger), it doesn't leave much room for nuanced responses to these socially threatening situations. But fighting, fleeing, and freezing aren't really appropriate options if you're getting up to speak at a business meeting or dealing with a painful accusation from someone you love. And when you don't spring into physical activity to deal with the threat, the body is left to stew in a buildup of neurochemicals, hormones, and physiological sensations, which makes returning to a balanced state much more difficult. Then, in turn, these physical experiences keep the mind and emotions activated. It's as though the mind says, "Hey, if my body is pumped, something bad must really be happening!"

Yet for this very reason, the body—despite all the discomfort—is actually an excellent detector of anxiety and can therefore be your ally in understanding your experience. As you begin to identify your own symptoms of anxiety and learn to bring nonjudgmental mindfulness to moments of anxiety, including being with your body in its charged state, you can move beyond reactivity and enter a realm of new possibilities.

The Brain on Anxiety

The threat-detection system is based in the amygdala, an almond-shaped mass that lies deep in the midbrain. It's part of the limbic system, a part of the brain that evolved early and is linked to both fear and the pleasure response. Because the amygdala's first job is to detect threats, it's always at the ready, scanning for anything that might put you at risk. This is great if you're in a situation where your life is threatened. But if you're just trying to get through a regular day—managing work, kids, your partner, pets, grocery shopping, getting the car to the shop, and on and on—the amygdala might not be helping you. In fact, it might be making things worse.

Importantly, the amygdala doesn't react solely to events in the outer world. While the gazelles' fight, flight, or freeze reaction arises in response to an external trigger (the approaching cheetah), we humans can have the same reaction to an *internal* event. So in addition to being activated by potentially threatening social situations in the external world, the fight, flight, or freeze mechanism can be triggered by a memory, a passing thought, or an interpretation of someone's behavior, which may or may not be accurate. For example, merely thinking a coworker is avoiding you can be a trigger, even though there could be a thousand reasons for your colleagues' behavior—most of them entirely unrelated to you.

It may be that some people are innately more susceptible to this kind of reactivity and that brain chemistry, hormones, and genetics all play a role in this. When this biological predisposition is coupled with the automaticity of the amygdala's threat-detection system, anxiety can come on with a tsunami-like rush, catching you unaware. One of the hallmarks of anxiety is this feeling of being ambushed by the suddenness of physical sensations, emotions, and thoughts that seem to have no outward trigger. In other words, you could be out walking the dog and feeling quite fine, then suddenly feel overcome with anxious thoughts and feelings about an upcoming event. In the middle of an otherwise neutral or even pleasant experience, there's a blast of physical sensations that have nothing to do with the present moment. Out of the blue, you're beset by a tightening in the belly, rapid heartbeat, tingly hands, and a rush of energy through the chest, along with a flood of thoughts and emotions, such as *I'll fail, I'm not good at this and never will be*, or *I should be more skilled* (all accompanied by feelings of discouragement or defeat); *That was a stupid answer* (accompanied by self-disparagement or self-loathing); or *I should never have taken this on. Who do I think I am?* (accompanied by self-doubt). These thoughts and emotions, and the sensations associated with them, are very uncomfortable and can create a downward spiral in which you generalize about your entire life based on a single, fleeting thought.

If this kind of internally aroused anxiety arises often—or even just a few times—you may, very naturally, become fearful of its sudden arrival, wondering if and when it will strike next. Of course, this feeds into the threat-detection system the fight, flight, or freeze mechanism is designed for. In this way, unwitting attempts to control the uncomfortable experience of anxiety can add to its power.

The Good News

All of this information about the biological underpinnings of anxiety may leave you wondering if there's any good news. In fact, there's a great deal of good news, starting with the fact that we are more than our amygdalas! Over the millennia, the human brain has evolved to also include the prefrontal cortex, which is responsible for executive function, reasoning, and higher-order decision making, all of which can help us choose alternatives to automatic reactions to threats, both internal and external. Furthermore, research indicates that mindfulness practice has a positive impact on various brain structures and functions (Davidson et al. 2003; Hölzel et al. 2010). And in regard to GAD and SAD specifically, research has shown that mindfulness practice can help relieve symptoms and facilitate behavioral changes (Golden and Gross 2010; Hofmann et al. 2010).

Although more research is needed to illuminate the mechanisms at work, it's clear that mindfulness allows us to interrupt automatic, reflexive fight, flight, or freeze reactions. By bringing mindfulness to our actual experience in the moment, we can intervene in the underlying processes and increase the likelihood of exerting more conscious control over our behaviors and attitudes. In so doing, we exercise so much more than just the brain; we also learn to work with our intention, wise effort, will, discipline, and the capacity to be kind to ourselves. These are all resources that can be harnessed and cultivated.

Like many people, you may wish you could fully understand the causes of your anxiety and root them out, as Mark, the young man at the beginning of this chapter, did. Unfortunately, searching for causes usually leads only to frustration and dead ends. But even here, there's more good news. One of the most powerful benefits of mindfulness is that you can effectively work to reduce anxiety's impact without having to know or understand its causes. In working with thousands of participants in our classes, over and over we've heard that mindfulness has changed their experience of anxiety—and their experience of their lives as a whole—without needing to know why.

Exercise: Identifying Your Symptoms

Now that you've learned more about the biological roots of anxiety, let's return to your own lived experience. Below is a checklist of symptoms divided into three categories: physical, cognitive, and emotional. Read through these lists and check off any that apply to you. If there are others that you experience that aren't listed here, write them in the spaces provided. Always attend to your own experience, even as you make use of information in the external world to know yourself and your experience more clearly and deeply.

Physical Sensations

_____ *Getting very hot or very cold, especially if this happens very quickly*

_____ *Rapid heartbeat, pounding heart, or heart palpitations*

_____ *Tightness in the chest or belly*

_____ *Nausea or butterflies in the stomach*

_____ *Shortness of breath or hyperventilation*

_____ *Feeling weak all over*

_____ *Shakiness or trembling*

_____ *Dizziness*

_____ *Dry mouth*

_____ *Excessive or unusual sweating*

_____ *Muscular aches or tension, especially in the head, neck, shoulders, and extremities*

_____ *Fatigue*

_____ *Other:* ____

_____ *Other:* ____

Thoughts and Cognitions

______ *Confusion*

______ *Racing thoughts*

______ *Thoughts about making a fool of yourself, not having it together, being crazy, being too sensitive, or becoming physically incapacitated (fearing fainting, having a heart attack, and so on)*

______ *Thoughts that express the desire to flee* (Let me out of here, I can't take it any longer, I just want to run away, I just want to die, I want it all to be over, *and so on)*

______ *Thoughts that express self-doubt, lack of confidence, or not being in control* (I can't do it, I don't have what it takes, *and so on)*

______ *Other:* ______________________________

______ *Other:* ______________________________

Emotions

______ *Panic*

______ *Fear or terror*

______ *Feeling sure that something bad is going to happen*

______ *Embarrassment or shame*

______ *Feeling criticized and rejected (especially if anxiety is frequent and help isn't available)*

______ *Anger*

______ *Depression*

______ *Helplessness*

______ *Hopelessness*

______ *A sense of unworthiness or losing confidence in areas where you used to feel capable*

______ *Other:* ______________________________

______ *Other:* ______________________________

Mindful Exploration: How Your Symptoms Affect Your Life

Identifying your symptoms is a great start. The next step in understanding your anxiety and building motivation to make changes is to look at how these symptoms are affecting your life. Take some time to consider the following questions and write your responses. Please be kind and gentle with yourself as you reflect and write. It takes a lot of courage to engage in this kind of mindful reflection. And remember, you're just beginning your journey with mindfulness. As you continue to work your way through this book, you'll develop a perspective and skills that will help you live as you wish, even with anxiety.

Do your anxiety symptoms limit your activities? If so, which activities?

____

____

Are there things you avoid doing, especially things you used to enjoy and get pleasure from, because of these symptoms?

____

____

Formal Practice: Mindful Check-In

The mindful check-in is a brief, three- to five-minute formal practice of moving attention away from whatever outer demands and experiences you may be facing and getting fully in touch with your internal experience in the moment. Think of it as taking a scan of the internal weather you're experiencing: noticing physical sensations, your state of mind and any thoughts that are arising, and any emotions that are present. You'll continue to explore these three realms—physical sensations, thoughts, and emotions—throughout the book. They provide a direct connection to your lived experience and are a resource that's constantly available during your mindfulness practice.

We highly recommend incorporating this practice into your daily routine. As you learn other practices in the following chapters, you'll see how the mindful check-in works with them.

As best you can, do this practice in a quiet space where you won't be disturbed or distracted. This might mean closing your office door, turning off your phone, or pausing in your car in the driveway when you get home from work. You can do this practice either lying down or sitting. If sitting, aim for a posture that's supported, balanced, and upright but not rigid. We recommend closing your eyes if you're comfortable doing so, but it's also fine to simply lower and soften your gaze.

To allow you to fully experience the meditation without referring to the book, we recommend that you listen to the downloadable audio version, available at http://www.newharbinger.com/29736 (see the back of this book for instructions on how to access it). However, you can also simply read the text below.

If you do, read through the entire script first to familiarize yourself with the practice, then do the meditation, referring back to the text as needed and taking three to five minutes for the practice.

Take a moment to appreciate yourself for giving yourself the time and space to do this practice. Amidst the hustle of our daily demands, it's rare for people to consciously and deliberately set aside even a few minutes to just see how they are. Most people are more apt to do this for a close friend, their children, or their partner. Turning this generosity toward yourself warrants some acknowledgment and recognition. With this small gesture, you're exercising a shift: resisting the tendency to just move along and instead making time and space to take care of yourself. You're making and honoring an intention to see what's really within you.

Now bring your full attention to the experiences of your body, your mind, and any thoughts or emotions that you're aware of, just as they are. There's no need to judge, analyze, evaluate, or assess your experience. The focus here is simply being with yourself fully, in the present moment, without getting caught up in mental or emotional preoccupations. If a tendency to judge or figure things out arises, simply notice that, then gently return to a friendly awareness of how you are. Continue directing your attention to the experiences of your body, mind, and emotions for about three minutes.

As your practice comes to a close, once again acknowledge your willingness to show up and be present to yourself and for yourself, knowing that, in this way, you're contributing to your wholeness and well-being.

Mindful Journaling

After your first practice of the mindful check-in, take some time to write about what you noticed: physical sensations, thoughts and state of mind, and any emotions, again with a sense of friendliness toward yourself. Here, and in all of the mindful journaling sections, we recommend not worrying about spelling and grammar; just write from your heart and describe how the practice went for you.

____

____

____

____

____

____

Mindful Exploration: Your Experience of Anxiety

This exercise will help you further explore your own lived experience of anxiety. While you might think you already know this state all too well, exploring anxiety in the manner outlined below is an avenue of self-discovery that can help you refine your understanding of and ability to describe what you actually experience when in an anxious state.

Give yourself some time to do this exercise in a place where you feel safe and secure and won't be interrupted, and please extend great kindness and care to yourself as you do it. Find a comfortable posture and begin by settling into the moment and your body, mind, and heart with a few breaths, perhaps even closing your eyes. Just allow everything to be without changing anything, as you did in the mindful check-in.

When you're ready, call to mind a recent experience of anxiety. If possible, choose a situation in which you felt only moderately anxious, not extremely anxious. That said, trust what arises, and focus on just one event. Let yourself get a full sense of the event, and then pay particular attention to what you experienced physically, mentally, and emotionally. Spend some time in this visualization, then read and respond to the following questions.

What bodily sensations did you experience during the event? Be as specific as possible. (For example, *I felt tingling in hands and my palms got sweaty. I couldn't focus my vision. My shoulders and the back of my neck were tight, and it was hard to breathe.*)

____

____

____

What thoughts or thinking processes were happening during the event? Again, be specific. (For example, *I had racing thoughts that were too numerous to catch. A voice that sounded like my dad's said, "Why would anyone listen to you?" Then I experienced a series of distressing images without words.*)

____

____

____

____

What emotions or feeling tones were present during that event? Here too, be specific. (For example, *I felt fearful of entering the room. I was worried about not being able to remember the flow of the presentation and feeling like a failure. And I was really angry that this was happening again.*)

____

____

____

____

When you've finished writing, congratulate yourself for taking the time to explore an experience of anxiety in such rich detail. This is an all-important first step in learning to turn toward your anxiety and transform your experience of it.

MINDFUL PAUSE

Before moving on, take a moment to pause and allow the practices, explorations, and information in this chapter to settle. The best way to work with this book is to go slowly, moving deliberately and with awareness. Like a gentle but steady rain, this allows what you're learning to soak in deeply. Too often, the speed of our daily lives encourages us to skim the surface and seek a quick fix. Mindfulness asks something different of us: to consciously slow down and simply let things be. Especially in relation to anxiety, this nurtures calmness at its biological roots.

Planning Your Formal Practice

In this chapter you learned your first formal practice: the mindful check-in. Please practice it daily for at least the next week. Because it's so brief, you can practice several times a day—as often as you'd like. Take a moment now to think about times when it would be helpful or convenient to incorporate this practice into your day. We encourage you to record these practice times in your calendar or to set an alarm or program a reminder on your phone to alert you that it's time to practice. Consider these to be appointments with yourself, and view them as being equally important as an appointment with a professional you're paying. When cultivating any new behavior, success hinges on setting an intention and then making a plan to follow through.

Using the following form, note each time you practice and briefly describe your experience. (For a downloadable version of the form, visit http://www.newharbinger.com/29736.) If you prefer other methods of self-expression, that's fine; for example, you might keep a journal with drawings that reflect your experience. The key is to capture the essence of this time you spent with yourself and what you noticed.

At the end of your first week of practice, take a few minutes to review how your practice has gone. It's typical for people to be filled with a sense of vigor and enthusiasm when beginning something new, yet it's all too easy for this to fade away. If your practice falters, remember your intention in working with this book. That intention to take care of yourself can help motivate you as time goes on. We're fond of the saying "What we measure grows." When you keep a record of your experience, willingness to continue the practice takes root. You honor and support yourself by recognizing your efforts, and you can make those efforts visible in a written log.

Mindful Check-In Practice Log

Day and time: ______________________________

Your experience: ______________________________

____

Day and time: ______________________________

Your experience: ______________________________

____

Day and time: ______________________________

Your experience: ______________________________

____

Day and time: ______________________________

Your experience: ______________________________

____

Day and time: ______________________________

Your experience: ______________________________

____

Day and time: ______________________________

Your experience: ______________________________

____

Day and time: ______________________________

Your experience: ______________________________

____

Closing the Chapter

Please congratulate yourself on taking important initial steps toward learning about anxiety and practicing mindfulness in this first chapter. This is difficult work, so extend some appreciation to yourself for sticking with it. In the next chapter, we'll provide an in-depth introduction to mindfulness, including key qualities of mindfulness, common obstacles, and practical pointers.

At the close of many chapters in this book, you'll find inspirational poems that express some of the universal truths of the human experience. They reflect the depth and fullness of being human and can illuminate the path toward greater self-knowledge, self-sovereignty, and wholeness. To end this first chapter, we offer a poem by David Whyte that speaks to the first steps you're taking in this journey and points to the power that lives inside each of us (1997, 37–38; reprinted with permission). This power is one of the reasons you're holding this book: something is calling to you, and you're choosing to listen.

The Journey

Above the mountains
the geese turn into
the light again
Painting their
black silhouettes
on an open sky.
Sometimes everything
has to be
inscribed across
the heavens
so you can find
the one line
already written
inside you.
Sometimes it takes
a great sky
to find that
small, bright
and indescribable
wedge of freedom
in your own heart.
Sometimes with
the bones of the black
sticks left when the fire
has gone out
someone has written

something new
in the ashes of your life.
You are not leaving.
Even as the light fades quickly.
You are arriving.

Chapter 2

What Is Mindfulness?

In the previous chapter, we explored anxiety, its underpinnings, and how it affects the mind and body. We also introduced a brief formal meditation practice: the mindful check-in. We've mentioned that mindfulness practice can play a vital role in transforming anxiety, so in this chapter we'll dive deeper into what mindfulness is.

Mindfulness is, in short, the practice of being aware of what's happening or what you're experiencing in the present moment. It's being here and now without judgment. This is a capacity that all human beings possess. Whenever you bring awareness to what you're directly experiencing via your senses, or to your state of mind via your thoughts and emotions, you're being mindful. When you really consider it, the only moment you can truly live in is the present moment—the very literal here and now. So why not be here now? This is where the rubber meets the road.

The Roots of Mindfulness

Mindfulness meditation comes from early Buddhist meditative traditions that originated over 2,500 years ago. Within those traditions, it's a primary practice for attaining peace and freedom from what enslaves the mind and heart—namely greed, hatred, and unawareness, which are considered to be the roots of all suffering, anxiety, and discontentment. Yet mindfulness is also a universal practice, found in many of the world's great philosophies, religions, and psychologies. Broadly speaking, mindfulness practice supports living a life of integrity, as well as the ability to gradually steady the mind and heart to help cultivate wisdom and compassion. This is a way of living that fosters greater ease and less anxiety, stress, and anguish.

Mindfulness-Based Stress Reduction

In 1979, Jon Kabat-Zinn, a molecular biologist with a doctorate from MIT and a long-standing personal practice in Buddhist meditation and hatha yoga, developed mindfulness-based stress reduction (MBSR) as a way to introduce these contemplative practices into health care as a form of participatory medicine. He designed his eight-week mindfulness-based stress reduction program to help people live better with stress, pain, and illness—in other words, the challenges of life. Through the years, this program has been extensively researched, and an ever-increasing volume of evidence-based research shows it to be highly effective in helping people who live with these challenges (Center for Mindfulness in Medicine, Health Care, and Society 2014). To date MBSR programs are offered in over 450 medical centers and community settings in the United States alone, and MBSR programs can be found on nearly every continent.

MBSR consists of a specific course of instruction in both formal and informal mindfulness practices and is informed by stress psychology, neuroscience, and experiential education within a group setting. The formal MBSR practices in this book include mindful breathing, the body scan, sitting meditation, loving-kindness meditation, mindful yoga, and walking meditation. Informal MBSR practices involve bringing mindful awareness to everyday activities, such as eating, communication, washing the dishes, working, and so on.

MBSR has been proven effective in alleviating panic and anxiety disorders in a study that followed up on participants. Three years after they completed the eight-week MBSR program, participants were still living better with anxiety (Miller, Fletcher, and Kabat-Zinn 1995).

Attitudes of Mindfulness

Certain attitudes are central to mindfulness, and fostering them will help you develop and sustain your practice. It's similar to adding nutrients to the soil to cultivate a vibrant and healthy garden. By attending to the attitudes of mindfulness, you can support your practice and help it flourish. And just as a well-tended garden bears seeds and fruit, so too will practicing mindfulness help foster all of the attitudes of mindfulness. By the way, in other books, you may find slightly different lists of the attitudes of mindfulness. We think the qualities listed below all play an important role in working with anxiety mindfully.

Volition or intention is the foundation that supports all of the other attitudes. Your intention, will, or volition is what sets you on the mindful path to working within yourself to gradually transform your anxiety and find more ease, freedom, and peace. By bringing intention to working with anxiety, you're developing persistence in seeing yourself as whole, capable, and resourceful.

Beginner's mind is an aspect of mind that's open to seeing from a fresh perspective. Meeting anxiety in this way, with curiosity, can play an extremely important role in transforming your experience. When you're willing to adopt another point of view, new possibilities arise, and this can help you challenge habitual anxious thoughts and feelings.

Patience is a quality that supports perseverance and fortitude when feelings of anxiety are challenging. Patience offers a broader perspective, allowing you to see that moments of anxiousness will pass in time.

Acknowledgment is the quality of meeting your experience as it is. For example, rather than trying to accept or be at peace with anxiety, you meet it and your experience of it as they are. You can acknowledge that anxiety is present and how much you don't like it, even as you apply patience and see anxiety as your current weather system, knowing it will pass.

MINDFUL PAUSE

With acknowledgment, you simply state the facts as they are, similar to how a meteorologist reports the weather. Pause now to give this a try. Take a moment to reflect upon a pleasant event and acknowledge how it felt. What was your direct experience of this event in your body and mind? Next, reflect upon an unpleasant event in the same way. Finally, reflect on a neutral event, again simply acknowledging your direct experience of it.

Nonjudgment means experiencing the present moment without the filters of evaluation. In the midst of anxiety, it can be all too easy to experience a secondary layer of judgment on top of the already uncomfortable anxious feelings. Stepping out of a judgmental mind-set allows you to see more clearly. When you let go of evaluations, many sources of anxiety simply fade away. When you feel anxiety, adopting a nonjudgmental stance can reset your mind into a more balanced state.

Nonstriving is the quality of being willing to meet any experience as it is, without trying to change it. With nonstriving, you understand the importance of being with things as they are—being with your experience without clinging to or rejecting what's there. (Note that nonstriving relates to your present-moment experiences during meditation and doesn't in any way negate the value of setting a wise intention to grow, learn, and change your relationship to anxiety.) In the midst of strong anxiety, the first response is often to flee or get out of the situation. If you can pause and really be with your experience without exerting any force against it, you gain the opportunity to know your experience more clearly and choose your response. You can also become less fearful of the physical sensations, thoughts, and emotions that accompany anxiety.

Self-reliance is an important quality for developing inner confidence. With practice, you can learn to trust yourself and your ability to turn toward your anxiety or any other uncomfortable feeling. In turning toward these feelings, it's important to bring other qualities of mindfulness to your experience, allowing the feelings, acknowledging them, and letting them be.

MINDFUL PAUSE

Pause now to reflect on a time when you turned toward an uncomfortable emotion. Maybe you acknowledged to yourself or someone else that a situation or interaction was difficult or painful. How did it feel to face the painful emotion? Did it help you feel you could face similar difficulties again with greater confidence?

Letting be or allowing is similar to nonstriving. It's a quality that gives space to whatever you encounter in the moment. For example, if anxiety comes up as you meditate, you could choose to work with it by allowing the feeling to be there. In time, you can learn to ride a wave of anxiety until it dissipates, just as a storm runs its course in the sky.

Self-compassion is a beautiful quality of meeting yourself with kindness. Yet, sadly, so many people are their own greatest adversaries. Most of us probably would never treat another person the way we sometimes treat ourselves. Self-compassion will naturally grow as you practice meditation. And bringing this quality into your experience of anxiety can be like being your own best friend in the midst of hardship, offering your hand in a moment when help is needed. As your self-compassion grows, you will come to know that you are there for yourself, and your anxiety will naturally decrease.

Balance and equanimity are related qualities that foster wisdom and provide a broader perspective so that you can see things more clearly. From this perspective, you understand that all things change and that your experience is so much wider and richer than temporary experiences of anxiety and other difficulties.

MINDFUL PAUSE

Pause for a moment to recall a time when you were standing on top of a mountain or other high point, seeing a panoramic view below. Your field of vision in that moment was so much wider than what you typically see at ground level. And in addition to seeing the beautiful view below, perhaps you also had a sense of how much more there was to see beyond the distant horizon. Take some time now to reflect on your relationship to anxiety from a broader perspective. In this way, you may come to know that it isn't the entire picture of you. There's more to see beyond this limited definition of who you are and who and how you can be.

Mindful Exploration: Trying on the Attitudes of Mindfulness

Take some time right now to slowly reread the descriptions of the attitudes of mindfulness. After reading each one, pause and reflect upon what it means to you, especially as you begin to work with anxiety. Take a moment to try on each attitude and see how it feels. As you do so, tune in to how you feel in your body, mind, and emotions. Finally, after trying on each attitude, briefly describe your experience, noting how it felt. For example, did it feel natural or easy to adopt a particular attitude, or was it difficult? If it was difficult, why might that be? Was the attitude unfamiliar, or did you feel yourself resisting it in some way?

Volition or intention: ______________________________

____

____

Beginner's mind: ______________________________

____

____

Patience: ______________________________

____

____

Acknowledgment: ______________________________

____

____

Nonjudgment: ______________________________

____

____

Nonstriving: ______________________________

____

____

Self-reliance: ____

____

____

Letting be or allowing: ____

____

____

Self-compassion: ____

____

____

Balance and equanimity: ____

____

____

TRY THIS!

You can practice mindfulness in two different ways: formally, as in the "Mindful Check-In" given in the last chapter; and informally, by bringing mindful attention to different activities. In the following experiment, you'll get a taste of informal mindfulness practice. Right now, take a break from reading and tune in to your body. Get up and stretch briefly, feeling your muscles and any tension. Next, look around and identify a little chore that needs to be done, such as folding laundry or washing the dishes. Then go ahead and do the chore you've identified, but rather than doing it mindlessly or on autopilot, as you might normally do, really attend to your experience. What information is coming in through your senses of vision, hearing, touch, smell, or taste? Does the chore bring up certain thoughts or types of thoughts? Do you notice any emotions arising? Perhaps it will bring up a memory and you'll find yourself drifting from your present-moment experience. If that happens, simply notice how the mind moves, and then, with gentle awareness, come back to the present moment.

Working with Challenges in Meditation

When you meditate, there will be times when you run into difficulties. Please rest assured that this is normal. In fact, it's so common that most meditation instruction addresses ways to work with these universal difficulties. The six main challenges that tend to come up are wanting, aversion, restlessness, sleepiness, doubt, and wandering mind. Even if you've never meditated, these may sound familiar—understandably so, given that meditation is a microcosm of the macrocosm of your life. In a way, just knowing that all the difficulties we meet can be boiled down to these six broad categories can be a great relief, especially as you learn how to work with them, as described below.

Wanting

Sometimes when you're meditating, your mind may feel anxious and you might try to find ways to alleviate the anxiety by feeling good. You may spin off from the meditation and begin to fantasize—perhaps about something as immediate as wanting to get up and eat a snack, or perhaps manifesting more grandiose desires, such as for a new car, a new house, or an exotic vacation. At this point, the mind has become preoccupied with seeking new delights. This type of wanting can become compelling and consuming, and at times you may feel a rush of desire surging through your body and mind, especially if you're feeling anxious.

When you become aware that you're in a state of desire, or wanting, you immediately have the opportunity to begin to change it. Mindfulness gives you a choice to respond directly and constructively to wanting, rather than fueling old patterns of reactivity. You can employ some of the attitudinal qualities of mindfulness, such as acknowledging what's present and letting it be. You can also open to self-compassion and equanimity and rest in the assurance that this too will pass.

Aversion

At other times you'll experience the opposite of wanting: not wanting, or aversion. In this state the mind isn't satisfied with what's happening in the here and now. Does this sound familiar? At a minimum, you've probably felt aversion for anxiety or things that cause anxiety. This can arise in meditation too, as anxiety or other unpleasant states arise in the mind. When this happens, you may have a strong feeling of "Oh no, not this again!" Here's where the saying "You can run, but you can't hide" comes in. If you always turn away when a difficult situation arises, you'll never get a chance to resolve it. This is particularly true of anxiety. If you don't turn toward it and learn that you can face it, it will continue to enslave you.

When you can recognize that you're in a place of angst and clearly see all the aversion you have toward that unpleasant state, you can begin to work with it. Becoming mindful of your anxiousness and resistance to it allows you to acknowledge what you're feeling and bring the curiosity of beginner's mind to it. The sooner you can detect your aversion, the better. That way it won't escape your attention until it gets so strong that it's difficult to manage. As you build your formal meditation practice, you'll begin to see the little ways in which aversion turns you away from your experience. In time, you can begin to transform aversion and feel more spaciousness and ease with whatever is happening.

Restlessness

Have you ever felt so restless or bored (which can be another form of anxiety) that you felt like you were crawling out of your own skin? Did you feel the need to do something—anything—to save yourself from that experience? If you tend to get restless or bored in your everyday life, this will surely happen when you meditate. However, restlessness is simply unharnessed energy, and if you can rein it in, you can use it to your own advantage, allowing you to settle into a place of greater calm and ease. That said, when you begin to meditate it's likely that the last thing you'll want to do is bring awareness to restlessness; instead, you'll probably have a strong urge to get away from it as quickly as possible. The problem is, whatever you do to try to distract yourself or get away from the restlessness can only be a short-term solution at best.

Mindfulness can be immensely helpful in working with restlessness. Once you become aware that restlessness is present, you can acknowledge the related feelings in your body and mind and let them be. You can learn to ride the waves of those sensations and the accompanying thoughts and emotions just like surfing waves on the ocean. As you begin to go with the flow rather than fighting it, approaching your experience with greater patience and self-reliance, restlessness will begin to dissipate.

Sleepiness

Feeling sleepy at times while meditating is very normal. Some times your concentration will be dull, and you'll feel listless or tired or have low energy. You may have the common experience that only when you stop to meditate do you realize just how tired you are. And in the midst of our hectic lives, we may not only become sleep deprived, but also find our circadian rhythms out of sync. Unfortunately, taking naps and the art of siesta are rapidly becoming faded memories of the past. Other factors may also make you tired. Anxiety can create a strong desire to not feel anything. The thought of going numb and just not be present can be enticing, because then you don't have to feel the anxiety. Though this may be seductive, it's also a trap. You probably don't want to sleep your life away!

Bringing mindfulness to sleepiness is the seed of one possible solution. After all, mindfulness is the opposite of sleep. Once you become aware of being sleepy, you have a choice to do something about it. You can open your eyes, stand up, and stretch or splash cold water on your face, then return to your meditation. You can also bring the attitudes of mindfulness to your experience. Use beginner's mind to investigate what's really going on. If you find that you're genuinely tired, you might want to bring mindfulness to improving your sleep at night. If you aren't genuinely tired, what is it that you don't want to feel? Perhaps anxiety, sadness, or anger?

Doubt

There will be times when you'll wonder if meditation is even helpful. Sure, you've heard that meditation has been beneficial for others, but will it necessarily work for you? You may also doubt your ability to meditate, interpreting the challenges of practice as signs of failure. It's common to feel this way, and also all too human to compare yourself to others and find yourself wanting.

Doubt will slowly recede as you deepen your practice and see how it helps with anxiety and distress. In time, you'll grow more confident and also more patient with yourself and the practice when doubt arises. In the meantime, the practice is simply to bring awareness and acknowledgment to all of your experiences, including doubt. By simply becoming aware of doubt, you're one step removed from it and therefore less consumed by it. Once you recognize that you've been trapped by doubt, you become freer from it and enter a place of new possibilities. When doubt arises, see it and acknowledge it. In time, as your practice deepens, doubt will subside.

Wandering Mind

Have no doubt about this: while you're meditating, you will, on many occasions, notice that your mind has been wandering widely, remembering the past, planning the future, and getting caught up in imagined scenarios. You may begin to attach to these thoughts and generate emotions based upon them. You may even begin to think this mind of yours has a mind of its own and is totally out of control! The good news is, this isn't a problem. In fact, it's a fundamental aspect of mindfulness: noticing the mind wandering again and again and returning to the practice. There are three key benefits to working with the wandering mind: it provides training in concentration, it helps you recognize unfinished business, and it illuminates how thoughts and emotions affect the body.

Concentration Training

As mentioned, repeatedly bringing the mind back from its wanderings is part of the practice in mindfulness meditation. Again and again, you'll see how the mind strays, and again and again, you'll bring it back to the here and now. Christian mystic St. Francis de Sales spoke to this dynamic in an incredibly compassionate way: "If the heart wanders or is distracted, bring it back to the point quite gently.…And even if you did nothing during the whole of your hour but bring your heart back…, though it went away every time you brought it back, your hour would be very well employed" (Levey and Levey 2009, 64).

This type of kind, gentle, persistent training primes the pump of concentration, and with practice, you'll be able to sustain your attention on the object of meditation for longer periods of time. It's like lifting weights; through repetition, you gain muscle mass. That said, a wandering mind can be insidious and will probably always be a factor to some degree. Self-compassion will be helpful. Remind yourself that you're doing the best you can, and take it easy on yourself. Also, be persistent. It's like an infant trying to stand and walk. If we gave up, we'd all still be crawling.

Recognizing Unfinished Business

Another benefit to working with the wandering mind is that it helps you recognize unfinished business and unacknowledged emotions. When you're meditating, you may notice that your mind repeatedly wanders into rumination, circular thinking, or painful emotions or memories. It may be that you don't fully realize how anxious (or sad, angry, confused, ashamed, or jealous) you've been feeling until you take time to sit still and be with yourself. This information is valuable, and you might consider it an invitation to address the issue. Remember, if something is coming up during meditation, it's also coming up in your life. The practice will show you, quite clearly, where you're stuck or holding back or what you're avoiding. By turning your attention to what is revealed, you can heal and bring your life back into balance.

Learning About How Thoughts and Emotions Affect the Body

Another benefit of working with the wandering mind is that it helps you see how your mind affects your body. This is the mind-body connection. There's a new field of research called affective neuroscience that's completely devoted to exploring how the mind affects the body. The good news is, you don't have to be a neuroscientist to observe this interconnection between mind and body. When you meditate, you'll see it quite clearly. Sometimes you'll realize that your mind has wandered off, perhaps into a feared scenario that sparked your anxiety. As you come back into the moment, you may notice that your jaw is as tight as a vice grip, your shoulders are tense and aching, and your stomach is in knots. This clearly reveals how purely mental events can indeed influence the body.

In the Face of Challenges, Persist

So that you won't get discouraged if your mind wanders or is sometimes filled with wanting, aversion, restlessness, sleepiness, or doubt, we want to reiterate that all of these challenges are natural and common. You're embarking on a training in a new way of life, and this will be a lifetime practice. The more you work with it, the more you'll get out of it, and along the way, these challenges or your perception of them will change. They can be your teachers. Bear in mind that, ultimately, the practice of meditation is about *you*. It's not so much about the breath or other object of focus; rather, it's a journey of discovery into the workings of your own mind and body. You can use the breath and other objects of attention to help settle yourself so that you might see your mind and body more clearly, but the reason for doing so is to understand yourself more fully, including how you get anxious, unhappy, or stuck. This is the path to inner peace and freedom.

Some wise words about the value of this exploration appear in the Dhammapada, an ancient Buddhist text: "Mind is the forerunner of all…conditions. Mind is chief; and they are mind-made" (Thera 2004, 1). This profound statement speaks to the importance of being mindful. Your mind truly is the creator of your own heaven and your own hell. You have the power within you to create either more anxiety or more peace in your life depending on how you perceive situations. There's an old Native American tale that speaks to this. It describes how we each have two wolves battling within us, one mean and one sweet. As to which wolf wins this battle, it depends on which one we feed. The same could be said for an internal struggle between anxiety and calm. So which wolf are you feeding? The good news is that your mind, and your relationship to it, is something you can influence. You can engage with your mind in ways that will help you make peace with yourself and the world.

Meditation Posture

Up to this point in the chapter, we've provided a great deal of background and conceptual information to provide a foundation for your mindfulness practice. Now, before we dive into the practices in earnest, we want to address a more concrete foundation: your meditation posture. Over the years, many people have asked us what the best meditation posture is. The answer is simple: whatever posture you can reside in that supports you in being awake and comfortable. This is the essence of the meditation posture: it facilitates being both at ease and alert. You don't have to be folded like a pretzel in a full lotus position, though of course you can if that's a relatively comfortable position for you to reside in for a period of time. The key is to take a posture that allows you to be present and comfortable so you can stay still.

You can meditate in a sitting posture in a chair or on a pillow or meditation cushion. To support wakefulness, you may find it helpful to keep your back reasonably straight, though not to the point where you're tense or rigid. Just like a finely tuned guitar has its strings neither too tight nor too loose, find the optimum position to create a harmonious practice. If sitting in a chair, we recommend that your back be a little forward from the back of the chair and both feet be flat on the floor. If you're sitting on a meditation cushion on the floor, we recommend folding your legs however is comfortable for you, being sure to keep both knees at or below hip level. Another alternative is to kneel on a tilted meditation bench or firm cushion, using it to support your hips.

You can also meditate either standing up or lying down. Standing is less common, but it's a wonderful option, especially when you're sleepy; it will help you stay awake and focused on your meditation. Lying down is also fine, especially if you have physical challenges that make extended sitting or standing uncomfortable. As you can see, posture doesn't really matter as long as you're present, awake, and comfortable.

In regard to hand position, you can place your hands on your thighs or lap, or by your sides if standing or lying down. As to whether your eyes should be open or closed, check this out for yourself and see what works best for you. Occasionally, people feel nauseous or dizzy while meditating. In most of these cases, the person's eyes were closed. If this happens to you, simply opening your eyes can restore your spatial orientation and get relief.

Mindfulness of Breathing

Breath and life are inseparable. We breathe constantly from birth to death, bringing in oxygen and expelling carbon dioxide. The average human breathes twenty times per minute, more than twenty-eight thousand times a day, and more than ten million times per year. This makes the breath a wonderful vehicle for mindfulness practice. It's always there, no matter where you are or what your situation; you can tune in to it at any moment. But the breath also has a couple of other advantages as a focus of meditation. First, turning attention to the breath can help settle or collect the mind and body. As you turn your focus to the breath, you'll gradually become calmer and more serene. In addition, mindfully breathing into your belly, sometimes called diaphragmatic breathing, can be extremely effective in calming an anxious mind and body. When you get anxious, your breath is likely to get more rapid and irregular. Intentionally directing your breath to your belly will help regulate your breathing, bringing you back into equilibrium much more quickly.

The second benefit of mindful breathing is that it can be used as an insight practice that helps you get directly in touch with the changing nature of life. Just as the ocean's waves ebb and flow at the shore, the breath constantly rises and falls, and it often changes in response to emotions or experiences. By observing this, you come to know and understand that all things change. Then, rather than putting your energy into fighting what's present, you begin to go with what's actually here and now, taking life one moment at a time. This prevents you from getting lost in the anxious thoughts related to the past and future, which is obviously very helpful in reducing anxiety.

Formal Practice: Mindful Breathing

To allow you to fully experience this meditation without referring to the book, we recommend that you listen to the downloadable audio instructions, which are available in two versions—five and fifteen minutes—at http://www.newharbinger.com/29736 (see the back of this book for instructions on how to access them). However, you can also simply read the text below. If you do this, read through the entire script first to familiarize yourself with the practice, then do the meditation, referring back to the text as needed and pausing briefly after each paragraph. Initially, take about five minutes for the practice. With time, you can extend the duration.

Please also remember this is a *practice*. Just as a musician needs to play an instrument regularly to become a virtuoso, regular practice is necessary to gain skill and facility in meditation. Also, please know that from time to time—or perhaps often—you will experience the challenges of meditation just discussed: wanting, aversion, restlessness, sleepiness, doubt, and wandering mind. In the face of these challenges, extend compassion to yourself and acknowledge that you're doing the best you can.

Hopefully you've been practicing the mindful check-in from chapter 1 regularly. If not, please return to chapter 1 and do that formal practice first, as this meditation builds upon it. Once you're ready, take a comfortable and alert position for this practice.

Take a few moments to welcome yourself to this practice of mindful breathing.

Now take a moment to gently do a mindful check-in, feeling into your body, mind, and emotions… Simply acknowledge whatever is present and let it be.

Now softly turn your awareness to your breath. Begin to find the place where you feel your breath most prominently and distinctly. It could be inside your nostrils, at the tip of your nose, or on your upper lip, or it may be in your chest, belly, or elsewhere in the body. You may even feel it in your entire body, as each breath enters and exits. Perhaps you're aware of an internal feeling of the body expanding and contracting, or you may sense your breath externally, through the touch of clothing that moves from breath to breath.

Let your awareness rest wherever the breath feels most distinct, and tune in to your breath, breathing in and out normally and naturally. There's no need to manipulate or analyze the breath, or even visualize it. Just breathe in and out in whatever way is natural in the moment. You may notice that the breath is sometimes rapid, sometimes deep, and sometimes in between. Just follow the natural rhythms of your breathing.

Breathing in and knowing you are breathing in… Breathing out and knowing you are breathing out. Taking your life one inhalation and one exhalation at a time. Being present.

There's nothing else to do just now, nowhere you have to go and no one you have to be—just breathing in and out with awareness.

There may be times when your attention wanders from the breath. When you recognize that, just acknowledge where the mind went and return to the breath, breathing in and out and being present. Just being aware of the breath moment to moment.

If you'd like to experience the calming effects of mindfully breathing into your abdomen, try it now, bringing your awareness to your belly and feeling how it inflates and expands as you inhale and deflates and contracts as you exhale. If you're unable to feel this very strongly, try letting your hands rest on your abdomen, feeling them rise as you inhale and fall as you exhale. Being present and taking your life one breath at a time.

As you come to the end of this meditation, take a few moments to congratulate yourself for devoting this time to practicing mindful breathing.

May there be ease and peace.

Mindful Journaling

Right after your first practice of mindful breathing, take a few moments to write about your experience. How did it go for you? What did you notice in your body, mind, and emotions? And how are you feeling right now?

____

____

____

____

____

____

____

____

Planning Your Formal Practice

In this chapter you learned your second formal practice: mindful breathing. Please practice it for at least five to fifteen minutes daily for the next week. As with the mindful check-in from chapter 1, we recommend scheduling your practice times in advance and making a commitment to keep these appointments with yourself. Then, use the following form to note each time you practice and briefly describe your experience (for a downloadable version, visit http://www.newharbinger.com/29736). If you prefer other forms of self-expression, that's fine; the key is to capture the essence of this time you spent with yourself and what you noticed.

Mindful Breathing Practice Log

Day and time: ____

Your experience: ____

____

Day and time: ____

Your experience: ____

____

Day and time: ____

Your experience: ____

____

Day and time: ____

Your experience: ____

____

Day and time: ____

Your experience: ____

____

Day and time: ____

Your experience: ____

____

Day and time: ____

Your experience: ____

____

Closing the Chapter

In this chapter, you learned a great deal of foundational information about mindfulness, including a brief history of mindfulness in general and the MBSR approach, the attitudes of mindfulness, and common challenges and how to work with them. You also learned a second formal practice: mindful breathing.

In chapter 3, we'll discuss the interplay between mindfulness and anxiety. We'll take a look at the role of the mind-body connection, perception, and patterns of habitual behavior and illuminate the difference between mindless reactivity and mindful responding. To open the door to this exploration, we'd like to leave you with a beautiful and inspiring poem by William Stafford (1998, 45; reprinted with permission).

You Reading This, Be Ready

Starting here, what do you want to remember?
How sunlight creeps along a shining floor?
What scent of old wood hovers,
what softened sound from outside fills the air?
Will you ever bring a better gift for the world
than the breathing respect that you carry wherever you go right now?
Are you waiting for time to show you some better thoughts?
When you turn around, starting here, lift this new glimpse that you found;
carry into evening all that you want from this day.
This interval you spent reading or hearing this, keep it for life—
What can anyone give you greater than now,
starting here, right in this room, when you turn around?

Chapter 3

Mindfulness and Anxiety

You may wonder how mindfulness can really help when your heart is pounding, your stomach is in knots, your thoughts are fixated on what might happen, and fear has a strong hold on you. That's exactly what we'll explore in this chapter. Building on the information we presented in chapter 1 about anxiety and in chapter 2 about mindfulness, we'll bring these two topics together and start to really get into the possibilities that open up when you practice being present with anxiety and attending to it with all of the attitudes of mindfulness.

Anxiety is sort of like time travel, as it typically arises when we focus on what might go wrong in the future. The human mind has a stunningly creative ability to conceptualize, fantasize, and plan, and it's all too easy to use this capacity to fabricate all kinds of terrifying scenarios that haven't yet happened and very likely may never happen. Some people view anxious thinking as a way to protect themselves: *If I can imagine the worst outcome, then I'll be better prepared to deal with whatever actually happens.* As discussed in chapter 1, this type of vigilance is a deeply ingrained survival mechanism. But as threats to our more immediate physical survival have waned, we've turned from scanning the horizon for danger to an inward focus, often fearing social consequences, such as the possibility of being overwhelmed, failing miserably, or being shamed. Anxiety thrives on these kinds of unpleasant projections into the future.

Turning Mindfulness Toward Anxiety

Mindfulness is a natural antidote to anxiety because it's a practice of attending to the present moment and meeting our experience in the moment with gentle acceptance. In this way, mindfulness has the power to help us form a new relationship with future-oriented fears. As we observe our reactions and fears and become more familiar with them, we can investigate elements of those experiences with greater care and objectivity. There's a great deal of power in becoming aware of how we perceive challenges, demands, and expectations.

Mindful Exploration: The Problem with Predictions

Take some time to look back and reflect on times when, filled with anxiety, you've anticipated or predicted dire outcomes. In general, were these predictions been borne out by your subsequent experience? Now choose a particular instance when you anticipated fearful future circumstances. Choose something that's already come to pass—perhaps a social event or interaction or a job interview or review. Whatever the situation may have been, spend a few minutes writing about your predictions, being specific and describing in detail what you expected would happen.

____

____

____

____

Continuing with this same experience, now write about what actually happened.

____

____

____

____

We're guessing that whatever happened was quite different from what you predicted. We're also guessing that the actual outcome wasn't as aversive as you may have feared. Whatever the case may have been in this particular situation, you may find it helpful to keep a journal of your anxious predictions. Then, for each, come back after the fact and describe what actually happened. This is a way of bringing mindfulness to both your predictions and your experience. With time, this exploration may help you develop more balance and equanimity in the face of fearful predictions.

The Role of Perception

Mindfulness practice is an invitation to be intimate with your direct experience—to know what's happening as it's happening, internally and externally. With mindfulness, you develop the ability to notice what you're noticing and can become aware of filters that color your perception of your experience. The amount of anxiety you experience may very well be tied to how you interpret the situations you face or fear you'll face.

Stress researchers Richard Lazarus and Susan Folkman have defined stress as "a particular relationship between the person and the environment that is appraised by the person as taxing or exceeding his or her resources and endangering his or her well-being" (1984, 19). Once you begin to see more clearly how you may be appraising situations, predicting dire outcomes, or imposing self-limiting concepts on yourself, you'll be less at the mercy of those thoughts. The old metaphor of the glass being half full or half empty points to becoming more aware of the way we see our lives, interpret our challenges, and acknowledge our gifts. You might view meditation as an invitation to "change the prescription of your glasses" and bring greater clarity to your perception. This puts you in a stronger position in so many ways, including allowing you to extend more kindness to yourself and bring more creativity and skillfulness to whatever you're anxious about.

The Limits of Control

As suggested earlier, looking ahead and anticipating the worst outcome is based on a desire for control, but any such control is, at best, an illusion. While reasonable planning for the future is necessary and can help ensure successful and productive outcomes, the stark reality is that we can never fully anticipate what we will actually experience. For example, consider this very moment, as you're reading this book. Do you think that a year ago or even a month ago you could have predicted the precise environment, mood, sensations, and thoughts you're directly experiencing in this moment? Of course not. Over and over again, we humans imagine what our lives will be like in the future, and over and over again we're humbled by the fact that we can never truly know.

On this thin ice, we are gripped by the force of anxiety, fearful of everything we can't control and imagining the worst. Although anxious thoughts are a way of trying to cope with and control the pervasive uncertainty in our lives, they tend to unleash a flood of uncomfortable sensations and emotions that swirl with ever-increasing intensity. The nervous system activates a complicated system of hormones leading to physical reactions that can further skew perceptions and lead to a crescendo of discomfort, fear, and anxiety. And in the midst of this chaos and cacophony, we tend to feel out of control, fueling the cycle.

But it need not be this way. While you can't precisely control your future experiences, you do have choices about how to respond in the face of fear, doubt, and anxiety. You can strengthen your ability to be more grounded and find refuge in your direct experience in the moment. And remember, this is the only moment in which you can really live anyway! It's also the only moment in which you can choose to respond mindfully, rather than reacting habitually. We'll discuss this at length shortly, but first, a quick experiment to explore how unified the experience of mind-body is and see how immediate and unconscious our reactions can be.

TRY THIS!

Imagine you're holding a lemon. In your hands, you feel the shape of this fruit. You look at it very closely, examining the details of its colors and textures, right down to the pores. Taking it to your nose, you sniff. Is there any scent? Now imagine that you cut it open, slicing it into wedges. You see the juice spurt out, the yellow pulp wet with juice. You lift a piece to your nose and notice any smell. Now you bring the lemon wedge to your lips. Touching the juicy pulp against the delicate skin of your lips, you anticipate what it will taste like when you place the lemon on your tongue.

What did you notice when you did this mental experiment? Did you have any bodily reactions? When people try this exercise, they often notice that they begin to salivate. Although there isn't actually a lemon, just imagining that there is causes the body to react.

Reacting and Responding

Now that you've seen how just thinking about a lemon can cause such a reaction, you probably have a better feel for how profoundly you can be affected by thoughts of feared outcomes. For example, say you anticipate that your colleagues will harshly judge an upcoming presentation you have to give. How might your body, mind, and emotions react to that thought? Or say you've scheduled a doctor's appointment because you've been having some unusual symptoms, and you keep thinking about the appointment and fearing you'll hear the worst. What impact might that have on your thoughts, emotions, and physical symptoms of anxiety?

Practicing mindfulness and being present with whatever is emerging in your experience, moment to moment, opens the door to interrupting these kinds of cycles of reactivity. When you can notice your experiences without identifying with them, this creates more space and less judgment, allowing you to become a scientist, curious about your life, rather than a victim of circumstances. With practice, you can strengthen your ability to recognize that a thought is just a thought, an emotion is just an emotion, and bodily sensations are just bodily sensations. All will eventually pass.

Just being aware of your experience in this way creates more freedom for you to ride a wave of unpleasantness and see it for what it is: a passing experience. You can begin to see thoughts of doom and dread as just thoughts and not necessarily predictors of what could happen. You can see emotions as just a form of energy moving within you, allowing you to experience even fear, worry, doubt, and anxiety with greater patience and equanimity, knowing that they too will change with time. And in the same way, you can see that unpleasant bodily sensations, such as a queasy stomach, sweaty palms, a pounding heart, or shakiness, will ebb with time, which allows you to hold these experiences with kindness and patience in the moment.

Of these three categories—thoughts, emotions, and sensations—thoughts are perhaps the trickiest. In a flash, they can hurl you into an uncharted universe of future possibilities that feel threatening and overwhelming, evoking emotions that unleash a flood of stress hormones. In such moments, grounding in the sensations of the body can be a place of refuge in the here and now. Whether pleasant or unpleasant, sensations can be anchors, keeping you in touch with the present moment with mindfulness.

Although this may seem to be a revolutionary thought, it's hardly new. As long ago as the fifteenth century, the poet Kabir advocated this practice of grounding in the body (2004, 27):

> Just throw away all thoughts of imaginary things,
> And stand firm in that which you are.

Standing firm doesn't apply only to sunny, happy times. It means being fully present even in demanding, difficult situations and tolerating the discomfort with both patience and kindness toward yourself. Intentionally pausing in the face of an urge to flee, fight, or freeze may feel like facing into a powerful windstorm. It is a potent choice and takes courage. As you take this stance, you can begin to observe your knee-jerk, automatic reactions to stress and anxiety. And in the rush of that reactivity, if you can pause, even for a breath or two, you can bring kind interest to your discomfort and awareness to your thoughts and emotions. As you stand firm, the agitation will begin to settle, and even just a bit of settling will open the door to more clarity and new possibilities for responding, rather than reacting. With time, you can begin to perceive similar situations through a different lens. You still may not like them, but you will be able to respond more skillfully.

Informal Practice: STOP

Here's a simple, informal practice that will help you pause and interrupt the vicious cycle of anxiety. It will be useful anytime you notice worried, anxious thoughts about projected future experiences or feel your body tensing with anxiety or gripped with fear. Fittingly, it uses the acronym STOP as a helpful way to remember to pause and be with whatever is happening as it unfolds.

S: Stop, pausing from the rush of activity.

T: Take a breath (or two or three).

O: Observe your experience of sensations, thoughts, and emotions and open to a wider field of awareness.

P: Proceed, or pause again, connecting with your present-moment experience.

Here's an example of using this informal practice: Ellen, a woman taking an MBSR class, returned from a full day at work and picked up her mail. In the mail, she noticed an official-looking letter from an organization that sponsored a conference where she was scheduled to give a talk. Seeing the envelope, she felt her muscles tense. As she opened the envelope and quickly read the letter requesting more information and setting forth deadlines, her heart started pounding and her hands began to sweat. She felt fear and had thoughts about having too much to do, not being able to meet these demands, and on and on. Then she saw how she had slipped into a pattern of reactivity. She realized that she was in the middle of a stress reaction, perceiving the challenge as a threat and underestimating her ability to manage the demands. She chose to STOP!

In that moment, she stopped, took a few breaths, realized what was happening, and understood that she needed to ground herself. So she chose to step away from the letter and do something completely different. She washed the dishes, looked out the window, and felt her feet on the ground. Next, she picked up the letter and reread it, and she was able to see it more clearly. The demands weren't so hard. She knew she could accomplish what was asked and provide the information on time. What had happened? Bringing mindful awareness to her reactivity opened the door to pausing and creating more space, allowing Ellen to respond differently, seeing something that had seemed overwhelming as actually quite manageable.

Turning Toward the Unwanted

Feelings of impatience, doubt, and self-judgment often accompany anxiety and can intensify the urge to push away or numb the fear and tension. Here too, making an effort to experience these emotions as they arise can seem counterintuitive, but it's a deeply wise choice. Trying to resist emotions only increases their intensity. Have you ever had an experience when you pushed away your feelings only to find them coming back again, begging to be known and acknowledged? Perhaps you're familiar with the wise phrase "What we resist persists."

In the end, denying fear, worry, and other unpleasant emotions won't bring you more ease. The path to surviving and even thriving in the face of these emotions is to turn toward them, especially when you're most challenged by emotions of doubt and dread and physical symptoms of anxiety. Each time you do so, you'll develop greater strength and skill. Of course, this isn't an easy journey. Along, the way, hold yourself with affectionate warmth, kindness, and patience. This will help foster acceptance of difficult emotions and allow you to tolerate remaining in contact with them.

As you begin working with anxiety in this way, you can calibrate the intensity by being gentle and fluid, moving toward and away from the difficulty in a way that's sensitive to what's working for you in the moment. For example, you can turn directly toward your fearful thoughts or emotions, and then, if need be, turn away again by redirecting your focus to bodily sensations not directly associated with your anxiety, such as feeling your feet on the ground, the temperature of the air, or the sensations of your breath as you intentionally breathe slowly and mindfully. Once you've become aware of and grounded in your bodily experience, you can turn toward challenging thoughts or emotions again. When you do, notice what's the same and what's different. In this way, turning toward your anxiety can also help you develop greater flexibility of attention.

Heartfulness

Here's a story that speaks to how we might turn toward our difficulties with warmth and self-compassion. In the early 1990s, the Stress Reduction Program had a classroom in the Benedict Building, an outpatient building of the University of Massachusetts Medical Center. This classroom was directly across from the Pediatric Outpatient Clinic. When a class was settled in silent meditation, we occasionally heard children's voices, sometimes chattering or joyful, other times demanding or sad, and sometimes protesting the treatment they were receiving. One day as the class sat in silent meditation, the urgent wails of a child pierced the room. Florence was aware of her body moving into a state of heightened alert, with a rapidly pounding heart and a powerful urge to run and offer assistance. Logically, Florence knew that this wasn't her job and that the child was accompanied by a parent and was being cared for by a professional, yet that immediate reaction occurred nonetheless.

When the meditation ended, the class participants discussed their reactions to hearing the child's urgent cry. At the next class, a participant brought a poem she was inspired to write, titled "The Crying Child Is Our Teacher." In it, she explored how everyone occasionally has an internal voice of a crying child, which we sometimes ignore, while at other times we rush to the rescue. She posed the possibility that perhaps the most skillful care we can offer this inner crying child is to patiently pause and turn toward the distress, hurt, and worry while offering ourselves warmth and love. Extending both awareness and tenderness to our challenges in this way is a path that deepens mindfulness and fosters skillful living.

In fact, the word "mindfulness" is often said to be synonymous with "heartfulness" because mindfulness is central to all meditation practice, just as the heart is central to the functioning of the body. Jon Kabat-Zinn has referred to choosing to practice mindfulness meditation, engaging intimately with our moment-to-moment experiences, as a "radical act of love" (2007, 13). While mindfulness can be perceived narrowly as only a form of attention, and compassion can similarly be seen as just a form of connection, they are actually two facets of the same force of awareness, which is innate in all human beings. As you develop the ability to pause and bring curiosity to your experience—especially when it may be uncomfortable—you increase your capacity to care for yourself more skillfully and kindly.

Formal Practice: Whole Body Awareness

With this formal practice, you'll strengthen your ability to connect with bodily sensations during easy or neutral times in your day, creating a foundation of body awareness that can better support you when you're feeling anxious. Because sensations are apparent only in the present moment, the more you can drop into your breath and whole body experience, the more you can stabilize your focus on where you actually are. With this grounding, you will be more able to notice the tendency to predict the future or ruminate with worry.

This practice invites you to begin with mindfulness of the breath, then expand awareness to your entire body. Sometimes when people begin to work with this practice, they become hijacked by worry or anxiety, perhaps because cultivating familiarity with the body is a new experience. Like any new skill, it will take time and patience to develop. If you find yourself beset by anxiety, there's no need to give yourself a hard time. Instead, simply notice and acknowledge the thoughts and emotions that are present without pushing them away, and offer kindness to yourself, knowing that this is quite normal. Then redirect your focus to the breath and body again. Even if this happens literally hundreds of times in a ten-minute session, that's okay. You're simply training, and retraining, your focus. With gentleness and firmness, just come back to the breath and the body.

To allow you to fully experience this meditation without referring to the book, we recommend that you listen to the downloadable audio version, which is available at http://www.newharbinger.com/29736 (see the back of this book for instructions on how to access it). However, you can also simply read the text below. If you do this, read through the entire script first to familiarize yourself with the practice, then do the meditation, referring back to the text as needed and pausing briefly after each paragraph. Take about twenty minutes for the practice. With time, you can extend the duration.

Take a few moments to welcome yourself to this practice of whole body awareness by establishing a comfortable and upright posture. Assume a posture that reflects your dignity and ability to be alert, whether in a chair or on a cushion on the floor. The intention you bring to your practice may include your wish to develop life skills for being more engaged and at ease. Cultivating an attitude of self-kindness can allow both discipline and curiosity to be filled with gentleness.

Now take a moment to bring focused awareness to the breath as it moves into and out of your body. Where do you feel this most vividly? Perhaps you feel it at your nostrils, where the air touches your upper lip, or as a swirl of air in your throat. You might experience the rise and fall of your chest with each inhalation and exhalation, or perhaps you feel this in your belly or more subtly in your abdomen. Perhaps you feel it throughout your body, expanding with each inhalation and returning to center with each exhalation. Wherever the sensations of your breath feel most available to you, rest in the awareness of those sensations.

Whenever your focus moves away from the sensations of breathing, gently but firmly return to the felt sense of the next breath. There's no need to condemn or judge yourself or give yourself a hard time. This is just the way the mind is... Steadily and easily, keep escorting your attention back to the breath, beginning anew again and again.

Now begin to widen the scope of your attention to the entire body, like shifting from a laser beam focused on the breath to a floodlight that encompasses the entire body. With this wider scope, you may notice more sensations—perhaps some at the level of the skin, and possibly some deep within the body. Even if your eyes are closed, you may be aware of light and shadow. You may notice scents, sounds, tastes in your mouth, or a range of sensations associated with contact, pressure, and touch. Simply note whatever sensations you may experience: pulsing, numbness, throbbing, expanding, contracting, warmth, coolness…whatever comes into awareness. As you receive the range of physical sensations, you may find that some are pleasant, others are unpleasant, and some are hardly detectable. With kind and consistent attention, you may find that the intensity of these sensations shifts with time. You are waking up to the richness of experience and constant change in the field of the body.

As you come to the end of this meditation, breathe intentionally and deliberately, feeling the range of sensations throughout your body. As you are ready, open your eyes and take in your surroundings. Take a moment to acknowledge yourself for participating in your own wellness, then stretch briefly before going about your day.

Mindful Journaling

Right after your first practice of whole body awareness, take a few moments to write about your experience. How did it go for you? What did you notice in your body, mind, and emotions? And how are you feeling right now?

____

____

____

____

____

____

____

Planning Your Formal Practice

In this chapter you learned your third formal practice: whole body awareness. Please practice it for at least twenty minutes daily for the next week. As usual, we recommend scheduling your practice times in advance and making a commitment to following through. Then, use the following form to note each time you practice, and briefly describe your experience. (For a downloadable version of the form, visit http://www.newharbinger.com/29736.)

Whole Body Awareness Practice Log

Day and time: ______________________________

Your experience: ______________________________

____

Day and time: ______________________________

Your experience: ______________________________

____

Day and time: ______________________________

Your experience: ______________________________

____

Day and time: ______________________________

Your experience: ______________________________

____

Day and time: ______________________________

Your experience: ______________________________

____

Day and time: ______________________________

Your experience: ______________________________

____

Day and time: ______________________________

Your experience: ______________________________

____

Closing the Chapter

In this chapter, we discussed how mindfulness can be useful in developing a new relationship to anxiety, creating an opportunity to respond wisely rather than reacting habitually. We took a look at the problem with predictions and also addressed the role of perception, the value of starting to see your life through different lenses, and the key skill of turning toward difficult experiences. You learned the informal practice of STOP, which can help you pause in difficult moments, and the formal practice of whole body awareness. You also learned that affectionate attention can support you in experiencing mindfulness as heartfulness.

You now have a foundation that will serve you well as you begin to delve more deeply into your experience of anxiety. In the next chapter, we'll explore how anxiety manifests in the body and how you can use mindfulness to meet anxiety in the body. The body is a reliable resource that can both offer information about how you're doing and serve as a refuge in times of turbulence.

Chapter 4

A Mindful Way of Meeting Anxiety in the Body

At this point in the book, you've deepened both your understanding of mindfulness and your experience of mindfulness. You've probably begun to get a feel for how it might serve you in working with anxiety. In this chapter, we'll explore mindful approaches to being with the body, highlighting how the body can be a source of information and wisdom in meeting anxious moments, and more generally, in all of the subtle and varied moments of your life. Will Johnson, meditator, bodyworker, and director of the Institute for Embodiment Training, speaks to the central importance of the body in mindfulness in his book *Aligned, Relaxed, Resilient: The Physical Foundations of Mindfulness*: "Mindfulness is not just an action of the mind. It begins with an awareness of the body" (2000, 3). In fact, we see tuning in to the body as a primary approach. It's a powerful way to bring yourself fully into the here and now, as sensations exist only in the present moment.

Coming Home to the Body

Given that we live our entire lives in and through the body, it's interesting that so many people don't spend much time actually getting to know their physical form. Of course, we might enjoy pleasurable experiences made possible by the body, whether through dance or sports, a hot bath, an intimate embrace with a loved one, a good meal, or the soft caress of a warm breeze. Likewise, we may tune in to experiences of pain or discomfort, typically with alarm. But mostly, people tend to have a perfunctory relationship with the body: feeding it, bathing it, clothing it, and maintaining it through medical and dental appointments.

Collectively, as a society, we tend to consider certain areas of the body—especially the space between the ears—as more important or special than others, such as the liver or spleen, toes or elbows. As individuals, we're likely to take pride in certain body parts and shun others. And overall, what we're more apt to pay attention to is ways in which the body doesn't measure up to our expectations or desires, whether an ideal of beauty or performance or due to pain, restricted movement, illness, or injury. People's relationship with their physical form is typically complex and fraught with this kind of judgment. There's a tendency to expect the body to function well, and when it doesn't, people may get confused or angry, or even feel betrayed by the body. This can certainly be the case with anxiety.

As you probably know all too well, anxiety can be an intense physical experience, with shortness of breath, heart fluttering, muscles tightening, head pounding, stomach churning, and other symptoms manifesting in a pattern that may be as familiar to you as your own signature. If you've been living with anxiety for a long time, it's possible that even when you aren't aware of feeling particularly anxious, you have an underlying current of physical nervousness, keeping the body ready to jump into action if necessary.

Given this physical distress, you might wonder why you would want to bring awareness directly to this bodily experience. What's to be gained here? First and foremost, it's worth paying attention to your physical experience because it's already present and you already feel it. And as you've probably learned, desperate attempts to push away unpleasant physical experiences typically makes them worse. Practicing mindfulness with the body is a radical alternative, turning toward the direct sensations that are showing up, rather than pushing them away. As discussed in chapter 3, this isn't done in an aggressive or harsh way. Rather, you investigate your experience with great kindness and gentleness, respecting yourself and not going beyond your current limits. Simply acknowledging the direct experience of the body, including how scary and strange it might feel to do this, is a big step that can begin to loosen the knots of anxiety.

Mindfulness training involves being fully *with* whatever is arising, recognizing that while you may not be in control of what's coming at you, by perceiving it clearly you can be more effective in meeting whatever comes up in any given moment. When you turn this kind of mindful attention to the realm of sensations, the body can serve as both a resource and a trustworthy partner in life. Knowing your body more intimately, and in an ongoing way, supports your capacity to meet all of your moments with more wisdom and compassion, including the anxious ones.

Meeting the Body Through the Body Scan

The formal practice of the body scan is a safe and contained way to hone your skill in attending to and being present with the body. This practice requires some willingness to move into the unknown and explore a different approach to the body than the more mechanistic perspective so many people have, or than the more avoidant or distracted perspective you may have adopted to manage your anxiety. Tuning in to the physical sensations available in your moment-to-moment experience of your body can be quite an adventure. It takes courage to really be with your experience in this way, but you will gift yourself with a treasure: reclaiming a way of being in your body and in the world that supports your life.

The body scan consists of systematically moving your attention through your body, bringing awareness to any sensations that are present moment to moment. It's not necessary to conjure up sensations; if a certain area is numb or feels hazy, that's fine—it's simply your experience in that moment. You can just note this and stay with the lack of sensation as best you can.

This formal practice gives you a lot to work with. First, you're directing your attention very specifically, bringing awareness to distinct areas that are sometimes quite small, such as the big toe, and other times quite large, such as an entire leg. This gives you a front row seat on just how flexible and responsive attention can be, narrowing like a laser or widening like a floodlight. Then there are the actual sensations themselves: tingling, pulsing, warmth, coolness, pressure, throbbing, tightness, fullness, emptiness, and more, from all-pervasive to exquisitely subtle, or perhaps no sensation at all.

As you attend to sensations in various parts of the body, you may notice emotions or thoughts arising. This offers an excellent opportunity to observe how the body and mind are interconnected: What emotions are evoked through the body? What thoughts or states of mind are arising? It's not necessary to figure out how or why this happens or to make logical sense of it. Simply being aware of the intimate connection between the body and thoughts and emotions is a pathway to awakening to the interconnectedness of your being.

It's especially important to attend to the attitude you bring to this endeavor, cultivating a stance of gentle, curious friendliness toward your entire experience. This approach, like a soft and steady rain soaking into the ground, can help your attention penetrate your experience more deeply without your having to push or make anything happen.

This attitude is especially important as you attend to areas of the body that might harbor pain, discomfort, or trauma. In the body, our history is immediate and direct, stored in the cells, tissues, and organs, and sometimes you may directly reexperience things when you pay attention to your body in a wise and loving way. Make an intention to bring gentleness and willingness to be with your experience, without pressure or judgment, as you engage in this practice.

Here's an example of how some of these aspects show up in the body scan. After learning this practice in an MBSR class, a gentleman in his sixties said, "It was so amazing. I could feel—without moving my body—an actual, subtle ache from an old knee injury during my football days. And when I turned my attention to my calf, the scar I have there, from where I got caught on a barbed wire fence when I was fourteen, throbbed a bit. It almost made me smile to think that these incidents have been traveling with me all these years and are present to me now. I also feel like there are things in my body that I haven't yet integrated, and they've just been waiting there for me to discover them and pay attention to them. And it wasn't just the scars and injuries. When I got to my chest, I sensed warmth and openness in my heart, which felt, in that moment, fully present and alive—not dependent on having someone to love or be loved by, but just an expression of who I am."

Formal Practice: Body Scan

To set up for this formal practice, choose a quiet, protected space where you won't be disturbed. Wear loose, comfortable clothing, and have a blanket nearby in case you get cold. Typically, the body scan is done lying down on a mat on the floor or on a firm bed. Another popular position for the body scan is the "astronaut" pose: lying on the floor with the hips close to a chair and the calves resting on the chair seat, knees directly over the hips. If lying on your back or the astronaut pose doesn't work well for you, any posture in which you can be alert and comfortable is fine, including sitting in a chair or even standing.

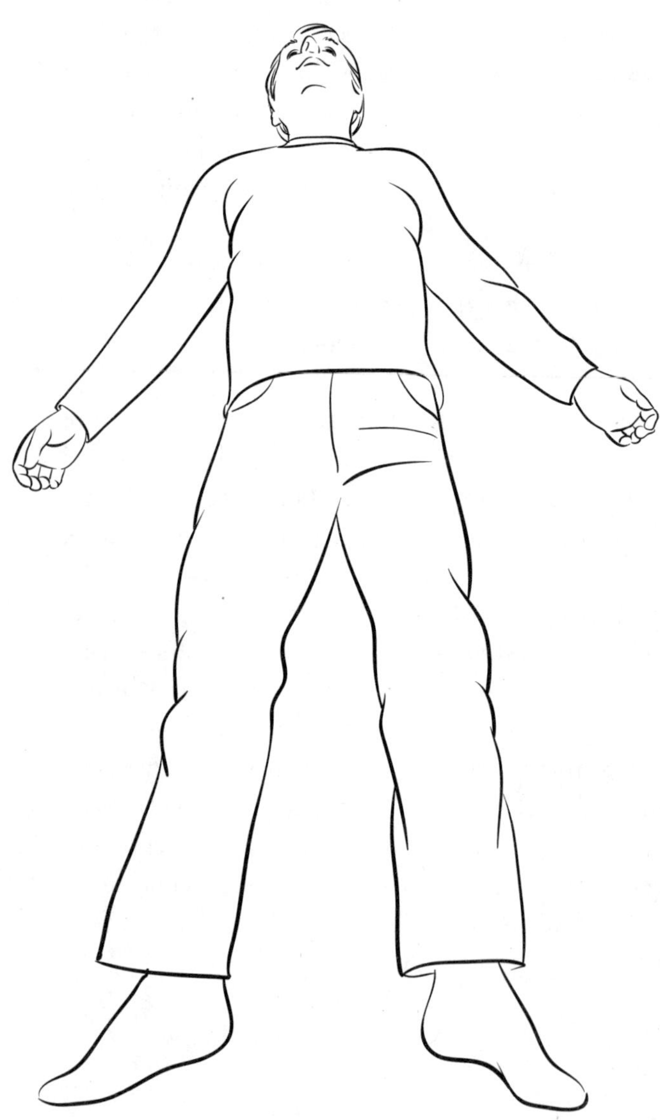

To allow you to fully experience this meditation without referring to the book, we recommend that you listen to the downloadable audio version, which is available in three versions—fifteen, thirty, and forty-five minutes—at http://www.newharbinger.com/29736 (see the back of this book for instructions on how to access these files). However, you can also simply read the text below. If you do, read through the entire script first to familiarize yourself with the practice, then do the meditation, referring back to the text as needed and pausing briefly after each paragraph.

If possible, take about forty-five minutes for the practice initially. Once you're familiar with the body scan, you can experiment with shorter times. Of course, if the longer duration is too much in terms of activating anxious states, begin with a shorter time. Whether you listen to the recording or read the text, it's a good idea to allot a bit of extra time for the practice so you also have some time to journal, rest, or otherwise just be with yourself afterward, allowing you to integrate your experience without having to immediately return to daily life.

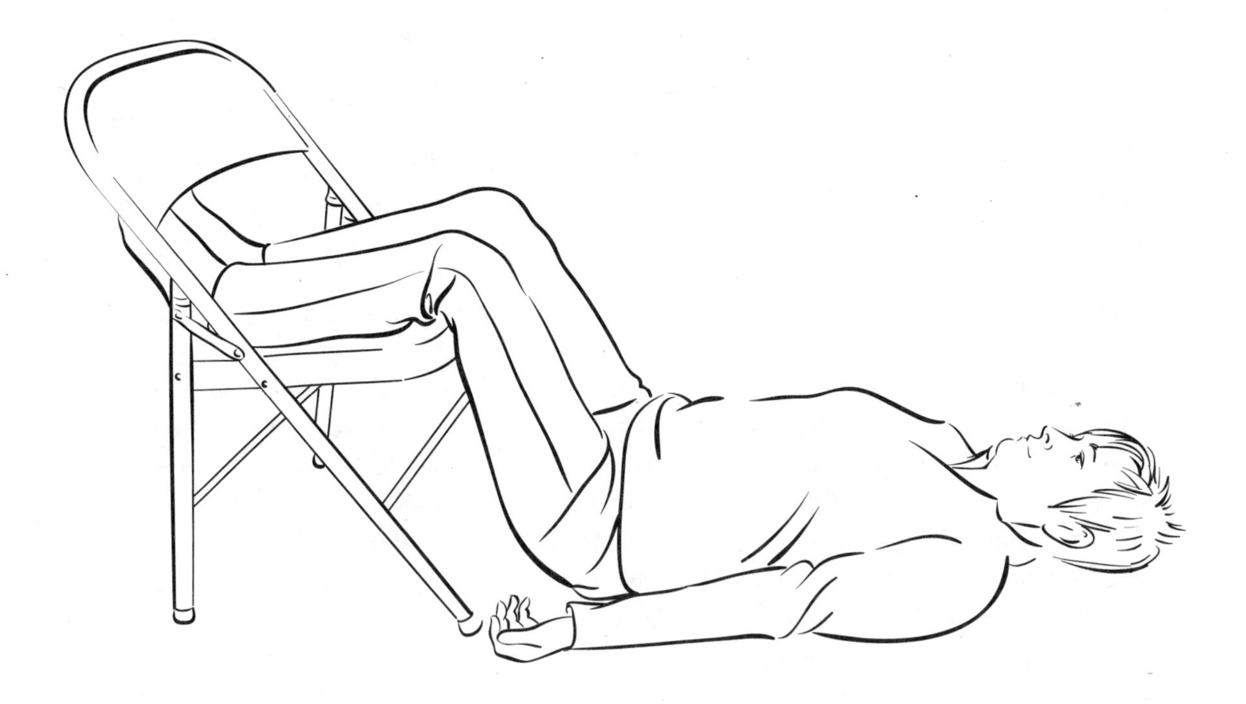

If your sensations or the emotions they evoke become too intense for you at any time during the body scan, use the breath as an anchor, stabilizing yourself with the sensations of breathing. Then, when you feel ready, return to the body scan, resuming with the region of the body where you left off.

Settle into whatever posture you've chosen. If you're lying down, let your legs be a bit apart, with your feet uncrossed and falling away from each other. Let your arms rest a slight distance away from the sides of your body, palms toward the ceiling if that's comfortable.

Begin to sense into your entire body: front, back, sides, core, and limbs… Feel the relative symmetry of your body… Settle into gravity, feeling the weight of your body.

Now narrow your focus to the sensations of breathing, especially the sensations of breath in your belly. To sense this more distinctly, you might bring your hands to rest on your belly and, without changing the breath in any way, directly feel the rising of the belly as you inhale and the falling of the belly as you exhale…not thinking about the breath, but directly feeling it as it's happening.

And now, returning your arms to your sides, shift your attention from the breath in the belly down through your left leg, thigh, knee, and lower leg, all the way down to the left foot where your foot is making contact with the floor or bed. Bring awareness to the experience of contact here and notice sensations of pressure. Then expand your awareness to include the entire bottom of your left foot: the heel, the arch, the ball… What sensations are present? Notice any tingling, pulsation, warmth or coolness, the feel of the air on your foot if it's bare, or the contact with a sock or stocking.

Now move your attention to the toes: the undersides, the tops, between the toes, exploring each individual toe… What sensations are present? Shift to the top of the foot and explore it in the same way… Then move to the ankle, encircling the ankle with your attention and feeling into what's present here… Next, move to the lower left leg, the calf, and shin, perhaps feeling the fullness of the calf along the floor, the sensations in the muscles, the weight… What's here for you?

Then continue to the knee—the kneecap, the back of the knee, the sides of the knee—perhaps feeling the way the leg is angled and how it's possible to know this without moving the leg… Now continue to the thigh, the entire region from the knee to the hip joint… Explore the sensations in your upper leg, from the surface of the skin to deep within, at the level of bone and muscle.

Now expand your focus to include the entire left leg from the top of the hip joint all the way down through the thigh, knee, lower leg, ankle, foot, and toes, breathing in and out as you rest with the left leg.

Now shift awareness from the left leg across the pelvis, then down the right leg all the way to where the right foot is making contact with the floor… Feel into this contact to whatever you can sense. Then slowly move up through the right foot and leg as you did the left, beginning by moving awareness along the bottom of the foot and exploring what's there… Next, bring your attention to the toes: the undersides, the tops, between the toes…exploring each individual toe… Moving on, direct attention to the top of the foot… Then move to the ankle, encircling the ankle with awareness.

Next, direct your attention to the lower leg, between the ankle and the knee, being awake to sensations here… Then rest your attention with the knee, feeling into what can be sensed… Perhaps you're aware of pulling or tension… Maybe you notice how your right knee feels different than the left… Being present.

Now move awareness up to the right thigh, front and back, inner and outer, all the way from the knee to the hip joint…feeling the fullness and weight of this part of the body and its contact with the floor. Now widen the beam of your attention to include the entire right leg from the hip joint to the toes…aware of sensations in the entire right leg.

Next, direct awareness to the base of the torso, the pelvis. Bring awareness to the lower belly, the softness of this area and sensations deep in the belly…sensations of digestion, pressure, fullness, or emptiness…and also attending to sensations at the level of the skin. Move your attention to the sides and back of the pelvis, to your hip bones and where your buttocks are meeting the floor or chair…sensing the entire pelvic bowl, tailbone, genitals, and anal region.

Now move up the torso to the upper belly: the area between the lower ribs and the navel… Perhaps you'll feel sensations of breathing here… Then direct your focus around to the sides, the waist area, and the mid back, perhaps sensing pressure, tension, or numbness…whatever is here.

Moving farther up, into the upper torso, sense the rib cage, the bony sternum protecting the heart, the chest area, the breasts…perhaps sensing the beating of the heart, coolness, or warmth… The heart is often referred to as the seat of emotions, and you may sense emotional tones here… What is it like to bring a curious, attentive friendliness to this part of the body?

Shift now to the sides of the upper torso: the sides of your ribs and your armpits… Then direct attention to the upper back and the shoulder blades as they rest on the floor…being awake to pressure or contact here.

Now open awareness to take in sensations throughout the upper torso. Then broaden your attention to include the entire torso, from the top of the shoulders through the chest and belly to the base of the pelvis…front and back…spine and organs… Suffuse your awareness throughout this core of the body, which houses so many systems of the body…breathing and sensing what can be felt here.

Next, narrow your focus to the shoulder girdle and then the left shoulder. With the beam of your attention, explore both the front and back of the shoulder, feeling directly whatever is here at this juncture of the upper arm with the torso. Now move down into the upper arm, feeling the inner and outer arm all the way down to the elbow. Then direct your attention into the elbow itself, sensing the bony protuberance and the soft inner fold. Then send your attention down into the lower arm, from the elbow to the wrist, exploring the sensations here... Next, direct awareness into the wrist itself. Perhaps you subtly feel your pulse... Now come to the hand: the palm, the fingers and thumb, the joints, the spaces between the fingers, the back of the hand...detecting any moistness or dryness, temperature, pressure, tingling... Being present.

Now widen your focus to include the entire left arm, from fingertips to the shoulder...breathing and resting in awareness of the entire left arm.

Next, move your attention from the left arm across to the right shoulder, being present to sensations in the front, sides, and back of the shoulder. Then move down through your right arm as you did through the left. Explore the upper arm, from shoulder to elbow... Then explore the elbow itself: the boniness at the back and the soft area of the fold... Next, move the beam of your attention into the lower arm... Then explore the wrist... Allow awareness to move down into your hand: the palm, the back of the hand, the fingers and fingertips, the thumb, and the joints. Bring awareness to how, without moving, you can sense the position of your fingers...exploring sensations in the entire right hand.

Now widen your focus to include the entire right arm, from fingertips to the shoulder... breathing and resting in awareness of the entire right arm.

Now move the focus to the neck, exploring the front, sides, and back of the neck and feeling sensations at the level of the skin and also deeper in...feeling into this area that houses the throat and the cervical area of the spine... Next, move from the back of the neck up into the back of the head: the scalp and the expanse of the back of the head from ear to ear. Then turn your attention to the top of your head, perhaps feeling the hair on your head, sensations of air touching your head, tightness, tingling...whatever is here.

Now bring your attention around the sides of your head to your forehead, temples, eyebrows, and eyes...allowing these areas to soften if you can. Next, direct awareness to your nose, cheeks, and jaw... Then move to the mouth, lips, and inside the mouth to the tongue and teeth. Next, bring your attention to the ears and the tiny muscles of the face, allowing all of the sensations in your face—the area of the body we most present to the world, the vehicle of expressing our feelings and words, and the part of the body that takes in the world via the sense organs.

Now broaden your attention to include the entire face and head... Then expand to also include the neck and shoulders. Expand again to include the arms and hands... And now extend to the entire torso: chest and belly, back and pelvis... Continue to broaden awareness, taking in your thighs and knees, lower legs, and finally your feet and toes. Hold the fullness of your entire body in awareness as you breathe...perceiving how your body is in this moment...sensing the completeness present in you as you are.

Rest in this awareness for a few moments. As you're ready, begin gently wiggling your fingers and toes. Then stretch, open your eyes, and gently broaden awareness to the world around you.

Mindful Journaling

Right after your first practice of the body scan, take a few moments to write about your experience. How did it go for you? What did you notice in your body, mind, and emotions? And how are you feeling right now?

____

____

____

____

____

____

Pointers for Practicing the Body Scan

There's no specific goal for the body scan, not even relaxation. Just showing up for yourself is all that's required. You don't even need to like the practice. Just bringing willingness and sincerity to being with your body is enough. The practice is simply to meet the body moment to moment and to work with your attention to the best of your ability—noticing when your awareness has wandered away from the body and where your attention went, and then coming back, with kindness and gentle firmness, to the practice. When your attention wanders, there's no need for judgment or blame.

You can do the body scan at any time: when you're feeling comfortable and at ease, and also when you're upset or agitated. Regular practice is the key. It's valuable to get to know yourself in a variety of different states. When you're first starting out, doing it every day at a set time will be particularly helpful. By showing up regularly to attend to your body, you foster a trusting relationship with your physical being. At the end of the chapter, we'll provide a practice log, as usual. But take a moment now to go ahead and set a time to practice daily for the next week, and keep this commitment to yourself. Think of it as a date with yourself—a date for extending care, consideration, and kindness to yourself.

As you meet the body in a regular and consistent way through this formal practice, you'll begin to notice that, like everything, sensations are constantly changing. Perhaps a tingle in your left thumb gets stronger or weaker. Maybe a numbness in your low back begins to wake up, first to a dull ache and then to an easing. Perhaps you'll discover that a clenched jaw can, with awareness, soften—not so much through effort as through consistent gentle attention. As you become familiar with the ever-changing nature of sensations—and, indeed, of your body itself—your sense of the fixed nature of your body will fade. In the same way, your sense of the grip of fear of anxiety may also begin to change. Your discoveries as you gradually deepen your presence with yourself will guide you to a new relationship with your body, your anxiety, and yourself.

Finally, bear in mind that the body scan isn't meant to be painful. If intense physical sensations or emotions emerge, if you're gritting your teeth or pushing through the practices, it's probably wise to back off. In this case, you may find it helpful to turn to the breath as an anchor or to practice the scan more briefly. If these difficulties continue, it may be best to seek the guidance of a therapist or counselor.

Using the Body Scan to Work with Anxiety

Here's a story that illuminates how the body scan works with anxiety. After a body-scan practice in an MBSR class, one woman shared, "As the body scan began, I was nervous that I'd become very anxious and not able to do it. As it turns out, I did feel some of my familiar anxious feelings, but they were only ripples. Even so, I was afraid that they'd get bigger. But it was almost like paying attention to my body softened them or let them calm down a little. They didn't go away entirely, but they didn't scare me as much. I also noticed that a lot of places in my body were completely fine—not anxious at all. That was a revelation. It makes me wonder how often I walk around thinking I'm anxious when most of me isn't anxious."

By bringing a gentle, curious, and friendly attitude toward your physical experience of anxiety, you can gradually shift your relationship to it. You can start to feel how it's like a wave, initially swelling, then cresting, then fading away. By learning, in detail, your body in different mood states, you can start to catch what's going on as it's happening, creating an opportunity to respond to your experience rather than reacting in an automatic way. This is the path to being more authentic and nuanced in your relationship with yourself in any situation that arises.

TRY THIS!

From time to time throughout your day, invite yourself to pause and come home to your direct experience. You might even repeat the word "stay" as an invitation to stop and dwell with yourself. Taking a page from Kabir, invite yourself to "stand firm in that which you are" (2004, 27). Another alternative in these moments is to engage in the informal practice of STOP, from chapter 3: stopping to take a mindful breath, open to and observe your experience, and then proceed with what you're doing, or pause again. However you choose to pause, tune in to what you notice in that pause and bring curiosity to potential subtle shifts in your experience. You may wish to write about this in your journal.

Meeting the Body Through Mindful Movement

Mindful movement can provide strong support in working with anxiety. Experiencing your body's strength and capabilities will inspire confidence in your ability to meet anxiety. In addition, directly experiencing your body, the container of your experience, as you move can help ground you when sensations of anxiety feel overwhelming. Yoga is an excellent vehicle for mindful movement because it's done in a thoughtful, focused, way, with attention to the breath. It also involves being attentive to your limitations, being sensitive to your needs and abilities, and exploring without pushing or overreaching. In this way, you can directly contact the strength and flexibility present within you.

The word "yoga" comes from the Sanskrit language, and we use it here in its most basic sense, meaning "to yoke." This practice yokes, or joins, the body and the breath, the body and the mind, the body and the heart—always with intention and awareness. It's a conscious uniting of your entire being in and with the present moment. Yoga is a recognition of the wholeness and completeness inherent in your being, and you tap into that when you approach the movements with that intention. In addition, the Sanskrit root of the word "yoga" is *yuj*, which means "to bind." We are literally bound to this body. When we feel distress, we might push against this feeling of being bound. Through the practice of mindful yoga, we can experience how this binding is a uniting field that encompasses and holds the jumbled experiences of anxiety. Like riverbanks that contain the depths and flow of a stream, the body contains the flowing sensations, emotions, and thoughts unleashed by anxiety.

While the movements in the following yoga practice and the standing yoga in chapter 5 are gentle and relatively simple, your own knowledge of your body and any limitations is more important than following the instructions here. Please let your innate wisdom be your guide. If something doesn't feel right for your body, it's perfectly fine to modify the movement or even just imagine doing the movement instead. If it's not possible for you to get down on the floor, you can do the poses while sitting in a chair, modifying the movements as needed. This might take some creativity, but the most important aspect of the practice is the sincerity and awareness you bring to whatever movements you do. If you have any questions about whether these movements are appropriate for your body, check with your health care provider. Ultimately, as with all of the practices in the book, the intention is to be present to your experience and learn something about what that's like for you, while also bringing a solid measure of kindness and self-care to the endeavor. If your body isn't able to perform specific movements suggested here, just do your best to engage the spirit of the exercise, modifying or omitting postures to support your own well-being.

Formal Practice: Mindful Floor Yoga

Choose a warm, protected space where you have room to lie down. Wear loose, comfortable clothing that's unrestricted at the waist to facilitate easy breathing. Having layers on hand is helpful, since the temperature of the body can change with the movements. You might also consider using a yoga mat or pad to cushion your body on the floor.

Some of the guidance suggests a breath pattern to support the movement—usually inhaling while lengthening the body and exhaling while contracting. However, feeling the breath and being in tune with your body's needs is more important, so if a suggested way of breathing doesn't feel right for you, experiment and do what works for you. The most important guidance in this regard is to be aware of any tendency to hold or constrain the breath and do your best to breathe fully. The breath is intimately connected to the mind and emotional state. Simply recognizing breathing patterns that are unconscious and encouraging the free flow of breath can restore ease and engender stability and strength. One final note: as with the body scan, mindful yoga is most beneficial if you commit to regular, consistent practice. Once you've learned the poses below, the entire sequence can be done in twenty to forty minutes. We've also provided downloadable audio instructions, available in three versions—fifteen, thirty, and forty-five minutes—at http://www.newharbinger.com/29736. Please schedule a time to practice regularly, perhaps alternating with the body scan.

Corpse Pose

Begin by lying on your back with your arms a short distance from your sides, palms facing up if possible. Lie with your legs outstretched, feet gently falling away from each other. If you need more support, such as a pillow under your knees, do what is needed to make yourself comfortable. This basic pose should feel familiar, as it's the same posture used for the body scan. In yoga this is referred to as the corpse pose. It's one of the most important poses, and one to return to between stretches. It allows the body to integrate the effects of the postures and also allows the mind and heart to be present to the body while it's at ease. The emphasis here is on alert stillness, the breath, and being fully present to yourself.

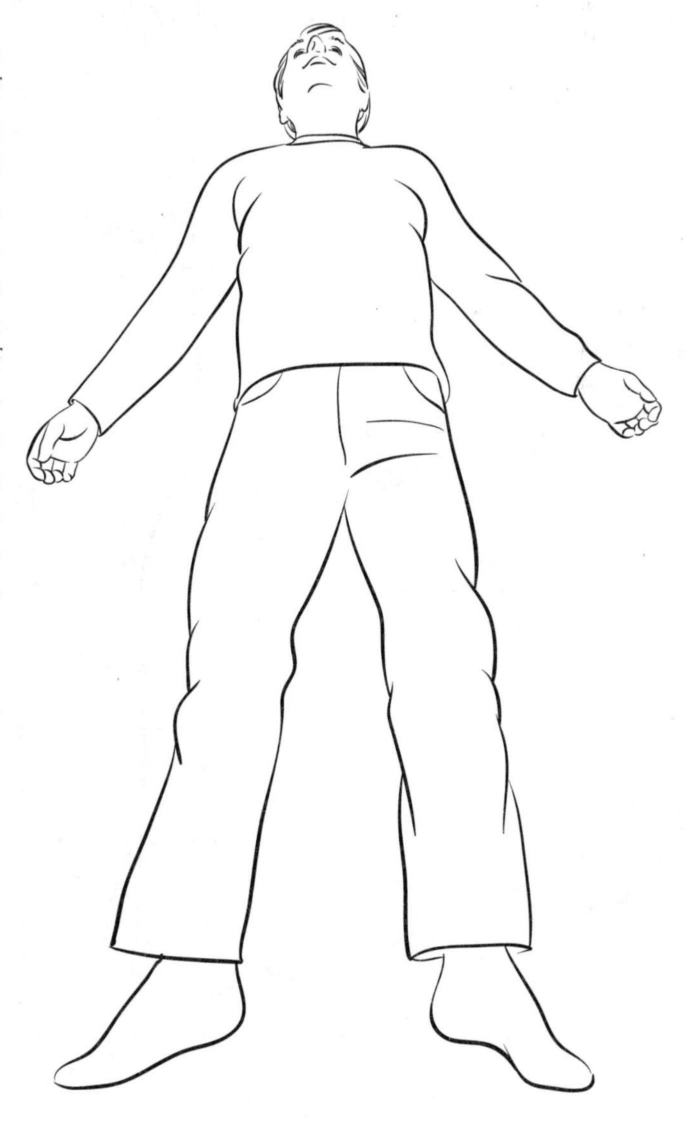

Long Stretch

On an inhalation, raise your arms overhead and stretch your arms and torso up along the floor away from center while stretching your heels in the opposite direction. Remaining in this stretched position, take a few slow, even breaths. Then, on an exhalation, float your arms down to your sides, feeling the weight of your arms as you move them through space. As you return your arms to the floor, notice how your entire body can release into gravity, taking support from the floor. Rest in corpse pose for a breath or two, then repeat the long stretch one or two more times.

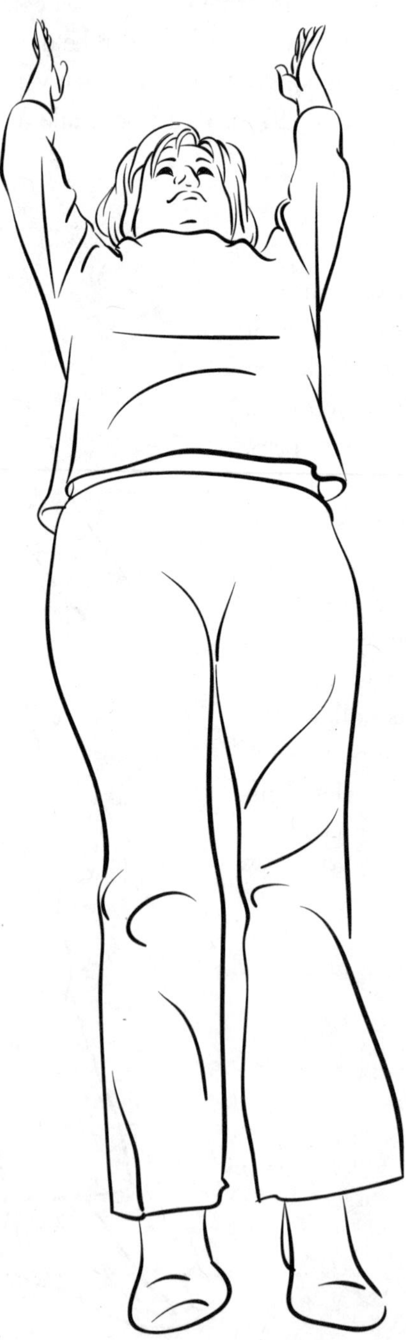

Pelvic Rocking

Bend your knees, sliding your feet up toward your buttocks and keeping them flat on the ground. Your knees should be pointed toward the ceiling. Tune in to the small of your back, which may have less contact with the floor than other parts of your spine. On an exhalation, press this part of your back into the floor, allowing the tailbone to tip up between the knees a bit. As you inhale, return the small of your back to the beginning position. Following the natural rhythm of your breath, continue the rocking motion, loosening and opening the lower back with this gentle movement. Extend your awareness to your entire body and notice where you may be holding any tension, such as in your shoulders, face, or hands. If you find any tension, see if it's possible to let it go, confining the movement to your lower back and the pelvis. As you're ready, return to corpse pose and experience the effects of the movement.

Knees to Chest

Draw your knees to your chest and hug them toward your torso as close as you comfortably can. Notice the feeling of your breath in this position, creating pressure along your abdomen and thighs. If you like, circle your knees to give your low back a massage against the floor. As you're ready, return to corpse pose.

Cat and Cow

Move onto your hands and knees so your body resembles a table, with your hands directly under your shoulders, fingers spread wide, and knees directly under your hips. If this position is difficult for your hands or wrists, form your hands into fists and rest your knuckles on the floor. Your neck should be in a neutral position, with the crown of your head pointing directly forward. As you exhale, extend the middle of your back up toward the ceiling while dropping your tailbone and head downward. This is the cat pose. As you inhale, ease the middle of your back toward the floor while extending your tailbone and head up toward the ceiling. This is the cow pose. Moving with your breath, repeat the poses several times, exploring the capacity of your entire spine for extension and flexion. Then return to the neutral starting position and remain in stillness for a moment.

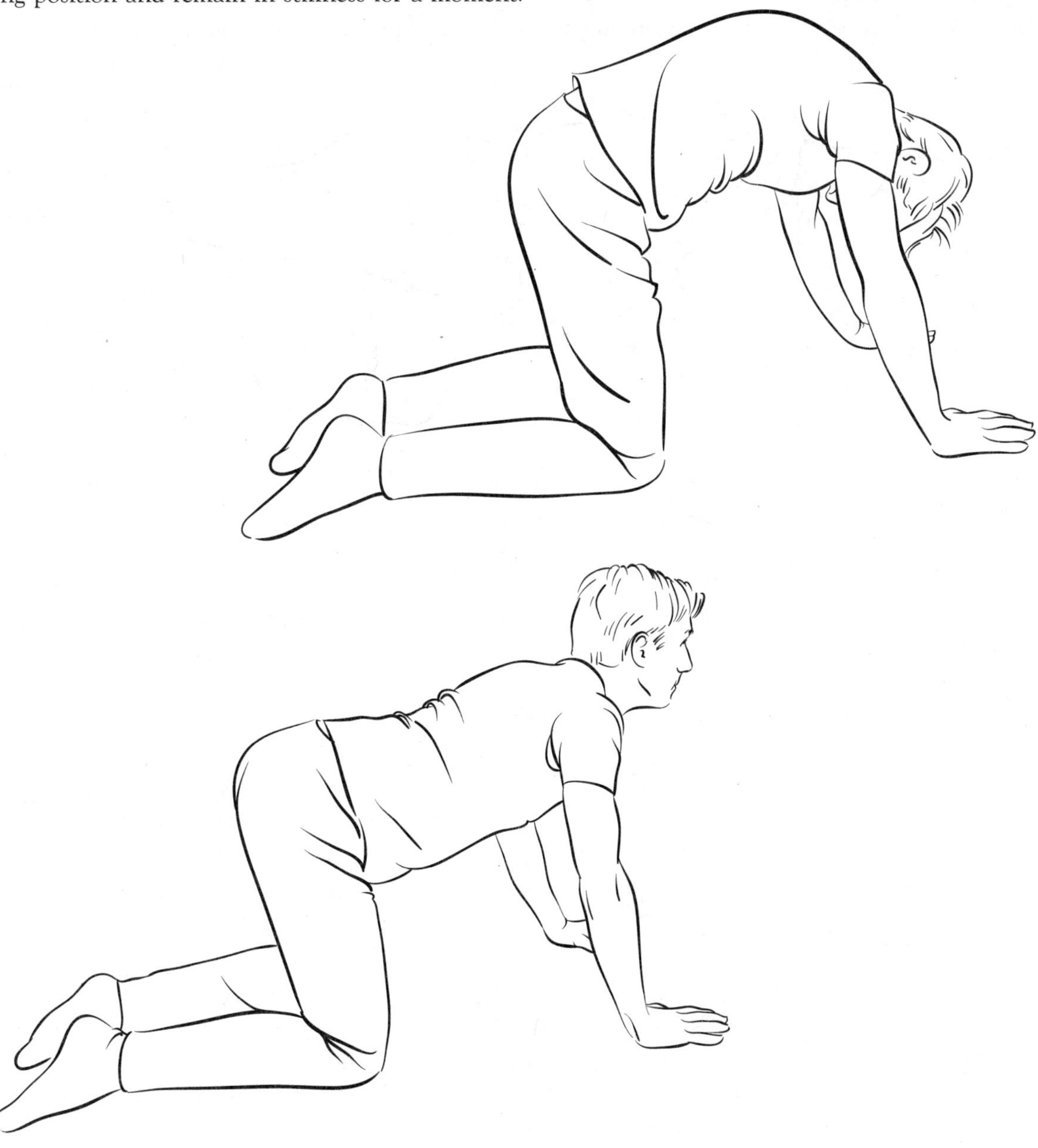

Balance Pose

From that neutral position on hands and knees, open your eyes if they've been closed and gaze at the floor in front of you to establish balance. As you're ready, lengthen your right leg, extending it behind you and raising it as high as you're able to comfortably, stretching through the leg and toes. As you're ready, stretch your left arm out in front of you, extending it horizontally from your shoulder through your fingertips. Feel the diagonal stretch through your body and the strength and supple dynamic of balance. Hold the pose—but not your breath!—for however long feels right for you, exploring the boundaries of your strength and balance. When you're ready, return to the neutral position. Then repeat on the other side, extending your left leg and right arm.

Return to the neutral position once again, then do a few more cycles of cat and cow to release the low back. When you're ready, lie down on your back once again and come into corpse pose.

Spinal Twist

Return to the starting position for pelvic rocking, bending your knees, sliding your feet up toward your buttocks, and keeping your feet flat on the ground. Your feet should be close together, touching in the middle. Extend your arms to your sides in a T shape if you have room, or clasp your hands behind your neck with your elbows bent and resting on the floor. On an exhalation, allow your knees to gently fall toward the left. Any amount of twist is fine. The soles of your feet may come off the floor as your knees shift. For a deeper twist, look out over your right shoulder. Take a few breaths in this position, allowing the twisting action to massage your organs and sensing the whole torso as it's twisting. Then, on an inhalation, bring your knees to center. On your next exhalation, allow your knees to gently fall to the right. If you like, look out over your left shoulder to deepen the twist. Remain here for a few breaths, then inhale and return to center. Repeat once again on each side, then return to corpse pose.

Cobra Pose

Roll over onto your belly and lie flat, with your legs extended and your feet uncrossed. Rest your head on one cheek or the other, or fold your arms so your forehead can rest on the back of your hands in a neutral position. Remain in this position for a moment and feel the breath, sensing your belly's contact with the floor as the breath flows in and out.

Fold your arms so your hands are directly under your shoulders, with your elbows close to your ribs. Bring your chin to the floor, then, on an inhalation, raise your chin, shoulders, and upper chest off the floor any distance that works for you, keeping your neck long and using your hands to stabilize (rather than lift) your upper body. Bring your shoulder blades together on your upper back, opening the chest, and feel the strength enlisted from your upper back. Gently press your palms into the floor to extend a little higher, but keep your elbows bent. Remain in this position for a moment, breathing fully, and then, as you're ready, slowly lower and come to rest. Repeat this pose if you'd like, and notice how your experience of the pose changes if you do it more than once.

Cobra pose activates the muscles of the upper back and shoulders and opens the chest area, countering any tendency to constrict through the chest and round the shoulders—a common habitual posture that can exacerbate anxious feelings. When practiced regularly, this pose supports a more upright posture and deeper breathing.

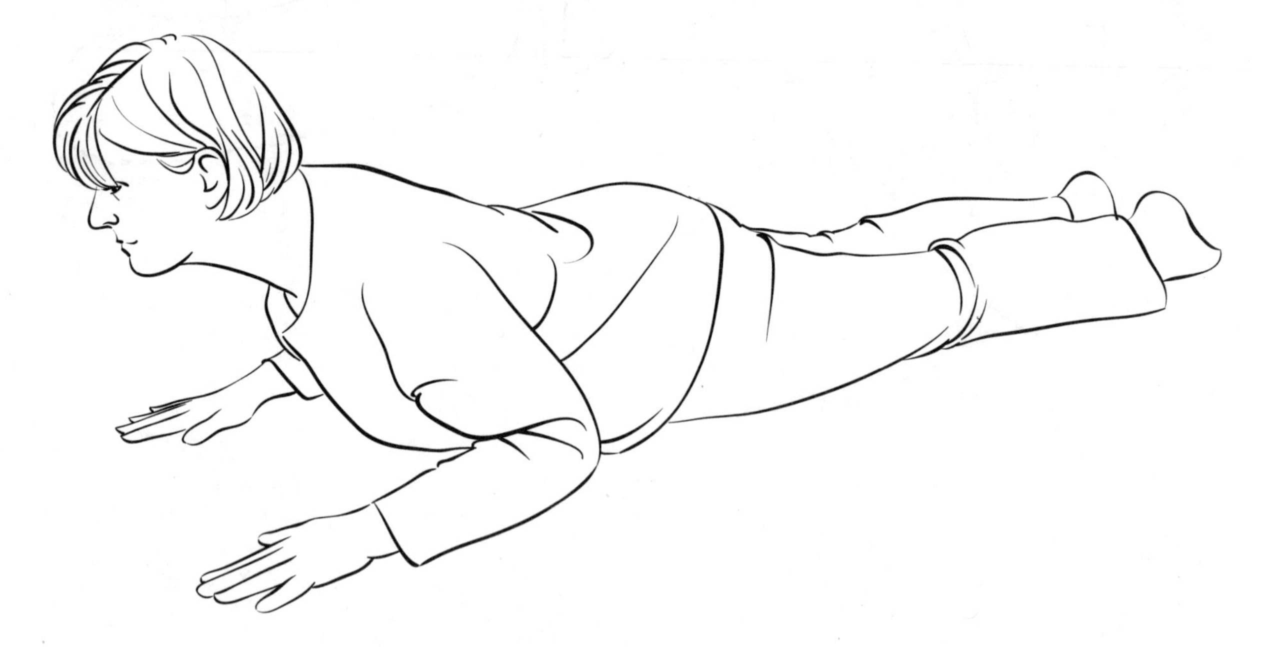

Corpse Pose

Roll over onto your back and return to corpse pose to finish the session, arranging your limbs in a balanced way and taking time to integrate all of the poses and movements and their effects. Rest in corpse pose for a few breaths, alert, awake, and present to sensations, thoughts, and emotions. Take a moment to acknowledge your intention and effort in this practice and congratulate yourself on your commitment to the practice.

Mindful Journaling

Right after your first practice of mindful floor yoga, take a few moments to write about your experience. How did it go for you? What did you notice in your body, mind, and emotions? And how are you feeling right now?

____

____

____

____

____

____

Informal Practice: Brief Body Scan in Mountain Pose

The body is always with you, and while you might not be able to roll out your mat at a moment's notice to practice yoga, you can use an informal practice of the mountain pose to quickly check in with your body at any point in time: before you sit down for a meeting at work, while watching your child's soccer practice, as you wait in line, or while sitting in a movie theater as the credits roll. Incorporating informal mindfulness practice into your daily life in this way is helpful for strengthening your practice overall and integrating what you're learning into new ways of being.

Checking in with the body can be done in just one minute or for longer, depending on how much time you have. And taking the mountain pose, a stance of stability and dignity, when you do so can serve as a physical prompt, informing you of your intention to bring awareness to your body.

Although mountain pose is typically practiced in a standing position, it can also be done in a sitting position. Begin by bringing attention to your feet or base; if you're sitting, this includes your feet and extends to your buttocks and hips making contact with the chair. The intention is to be well grounded, balanced, and upright, but not rigid. Your knees should feel easy, not locked, and your shoulders should be over your hips. Allow your head to balance lightly at the top of your spine. Let your arms hang from your shoulders, with your shoulder girdle relaxed and broad and your chest gently opening. You need not close your eyes, but do soften your face, eyes, jaw, and forehead. In this position, briefly scan through your entire body, making space for whatever is there, noting sensations, and simply being present to the whole body.

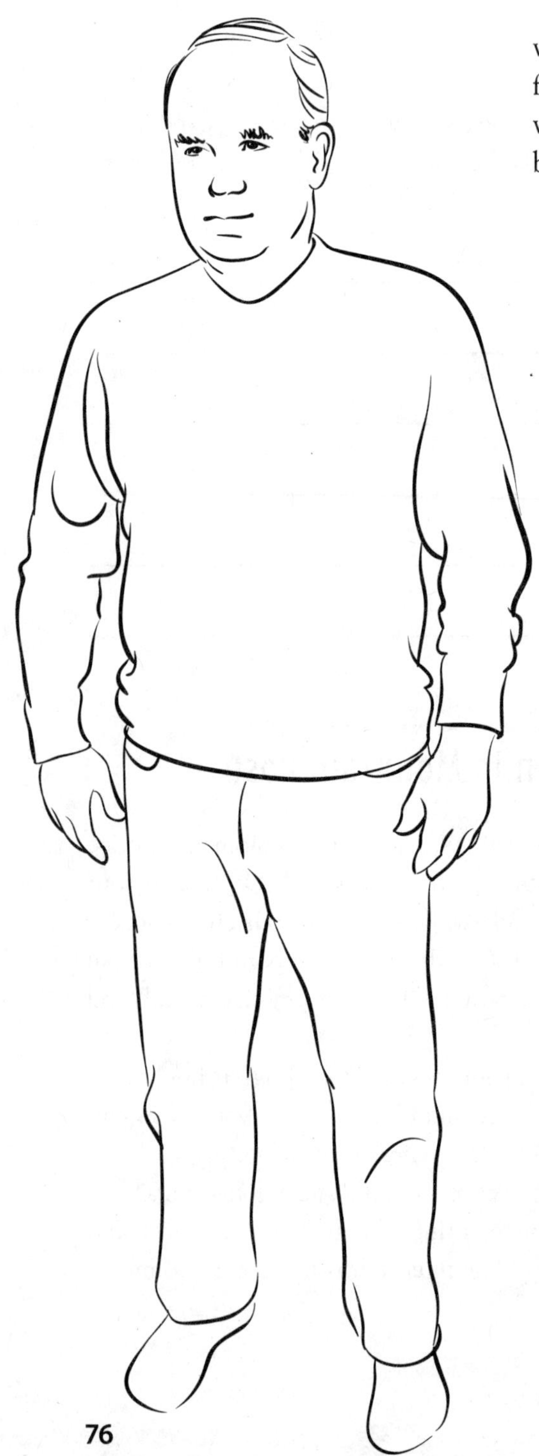

You can do this informal practice anytime you think of it: when you feel the thrum of anxiety starting up, when you're feeling joyful, when you're feeling down, when you're tired, and when you're energized. In other words, keep checking in with the body to explore all of the ways you are.

Planning Your Formal Practice

In this chapter you learned two new formal practices: the body scan and mindful floor yoga. Please practice them daily for the next week, perhaps alternating which one you practice from day to day. It's fine to add any of the previous practices as well, but for the next week, be sure to practice those in this chapter. As usual, we recommend scheduling your practice times in advance and making a commitment to keep these appointments with yourself. Then, use the following form to note each time you practice and briefly describe your experience (visit http://www.newharbinger.com/29736 for a downloadable version).

Body Scan and Mindful Floor Yoga Practice Log

Day and time: ______________________________

Your experience: ______________________________

____

Day and time: ______________________________

Your experience: ______________________________

____

Day and time: ______________________________

Your experience: ______________________________

____

Day and time: ______________________________

Your experience: ______________________________

____

Day and time: ______________________________

Your experience: ______________________________

____

Day and time: ____

Your experience: ____

____

Day and time: ____

Your experience: ____

____

Closing the Chapter

As you come to the end of this chapter, take some time to recognize and appreciate how you're attending to and caring for yourself. Congratulate yourself for the active role you're taking to support your health and well-being both in relation to your anxiety and in relation to your life as a whole. We trust that you're discovering that you are more than your anxiety, and that the body-oriented practices in this chapter have put you more closely in touch with your inner resilience. Through continued practice, this inner resilience will grow.

Now that you've learned some practices that can help you come home to your body and be more sensitive to the signals it's sending about your overall state, you have a good foundation for the work in the next chapter: meeting anxious thoughts with mindfulness. But before you read on, take some time to reflect upon the following poem by Danna Faulds (2009, 30; reprinted with permission). It speaks beautifully to the power and potential that lie in turning toward the body, even when sensations are challenging.

Nothing More Is Needed

Inside the hot, hard knot of raw sensation,
here inside the heart of fear and pain,
I find the flame of truth
My path is through—
diving right into whatever past conditioning
bids me hide or push aside.
When I soften, open, accept, and receive,
the flow of energy is immediate.
Nothing more is needed to awaken completely
than the intimate experience of now.

Chapter 5

A Mindful Way of Meeting Anxious Thoughts

For centuries, if not millennia, people have understood the connection between thoughts and various forms of emotional suffering, including anxiety. As long ago as 1647, John Milton wrote in *Paradise Lost*, "The mind is its own place and in itself can make a heaven of hell, a hell of heaven" (2005, 17). What Milton refers to as "the mind" is the constant narrative formed by streaming of thoughts, and the nature of that stream of thoughts has a great deal to do with the quality of your daily living. Thoughts have the potential to make a heaven of hell when they are curious, creative, positive, and engaged with learning. And conversely, they can make a hell of heaven when they are filled with anxiety, fearful predictions, self-criticism, and other forms of negativity. Either way, we humans tend to closely identify with our thoughts, creating an abstract and often unfounded reality.

With mindfulness, you can forge a more fluid, kind, and gracious relationship with who you are at all levels: sensations, thoughts, and emotions. Unfortunately, this tends to be discouraged by our culture in general, which holds tightly to René Descartes's enduring statement "I think, therefore I am" (1999, 25). This statement has influenced generations of Westerners to believe that thinking is how one knows one is truly alive. Actually, it would be more accurate if reversed: "I am, therefore thinking happens." Understanding and exploring new ways to relate to thoughts is a key strategy for easing anxiety. A woman who suffered from panic attacks and was taking the MBSR program once put it like this: "I didn't know I was more than my thinking! Knowing and experiencing this has widened my understanding of who I am, and I feel freer."

Thinking Happens

To understand how inextricably thinking and anxiety are intertwined, consider this: Thinking is at work anytime you imagine, or predict the future. It's at work anytime you catastrophize, assuming that the worst possible outcome will come to pass. In this way, it plays a leading role in triggering and maintaining anxiety, which arises as you grapple with unease about the future—a future that you can't truly know and probably can't control. Most people, even those who aren't plagued by anxiety, spend a great deal of energy strategizing ways to escape the discomfort of living with ambiguity and uncertainty. And for those who are plagued by anxiety, thoughts about dreaded outcomes, future embarrassment or failure, judgment, and shame contribute to fearful emotions and uncomfortable bodily reactions—the many symptoms of anxiety outlined in chapter 1. A big part of the solution to this problem is learning to identify anxious thoughts as merely thoughts, not reality.

As discussed in the previous chapter, tuning in to the totality of your bodily experience, or tuning in to your body in motion, can help you calm and settle yourself. Through meditation, you can also begin to work with thoughts directly. When first beginning your meditation practice, you may find that thinking and being aware of thoughts is a delicate process. Beginning meditators often notice how very busy the mind is, sometimes feeling like a radio with fifteen channels on at the same time, all at full volume. Another metaphor used to describe the erratic and frenetic nature of thoughts is a monkey swinging restlessly from branch to branch and never stopping. Yet another metaphor for this kind of mind activity is a rushing train of thoughts, each car streaming forward and pulling along another car of thought. A sexual fantasy is followed by planning tomorrow's meeting, followed by a daydream about an upcoming vacation, followed by a judgmental thought about a coworker, followed by an anxious thought about a medical test, and on and on.

When you cultivate moment-to-moment awareness through mindfulness practice, you develop the capacity to see that train of thought clearly, to slow that monkey down, and to turn down some of those channels on the radio—or turn them off completely. You learn that you have thoughts but are more than those thoughts. You can begin to see the space between the cars in your train of thought, the sky above, and the ground beneath. You begin to experience your thinking from a wider perspective. The fullness of being alive encompasses thinking—and so much more than thinking.

By progressively developing steadier attention and closer observation of your internal processes, you can begin to experience the constant flow of change at all levels of your being: bodily sensations, emotions, and thoughts. And as you develop the various attitudes of mindfulness outlined in chapter 2, you can increasingly accept whatever arises in your experience from moment to moment. In this way, you can more courageously and kindly abide with anxious feelings, bringing curiosity and interest to the ongoing interplay between emotions, thoughts, and bodily sensations. Just stopping to be with the intensity of an anxious situation offers you more space, clarity, and leverage to work with the situation wisely.

MINDFUL PAUSE

Pause for a moment and connect with your body. Check in to see what sensations are present just now. As you settle into your body and this mindful pause, turn your attention to any thinking that's occurring. What do you notice? Can you identify specific thoughts? Do certain types of thoughts predominate? What thoughts are strongest? Are you planning or worrying? Are you mulling over something from the past? Are you appreciating your experience in the moment? Are you simply noting your experience in an objective way?

Examining Thoughts

Since the content of thoughts has a great deal to do with how anxious you may be in any given situation, let's take a closer look at thoughts themselves. The emergence of thought is a mysterious process that isn't totally within your control. The current prevailing belief is that thoughts are emitted from the brain just as digestive enzymes are emitted from the stomach or saliva is produced in the mouth. Have you ever had the experience of being totally surprised by what you just thought? Even when you aim your attention and choose to focus on one object or activity, your mind will continue to deliver unrelated thoughts and move in surprising ways—ways you could never predict. Being aware of this propensity of the brain to engage in seemingly random patterns of thinking can help you be interested and curious in your thoughts without taking them all to be accurate. With practice, mindfulness allows you to see when you're caught up in thinking versus when you're aware of your ongoing stream of thought without taking it so seriously. Recognizing this and developing the ability to shift into the latter perspective is particularly important in working with patterns of anxious thoughts, beliefs, and predictions.

Early childhood experiences may have played a role in the kinds of thought patterns that are common for you now. Growing up in a family that valued intellectual curiosity versus a family that tended to pit people against one another versus a family where displays of emotion were discouraged—each can create an environment that supports the development of certain patterns of thinking. If you were judged harshly as a child, you might tend to be judgmental as an adult. If you grew up under pressure to behave perfectly and always excel, you could develop a pattern of striving that leads to physical, emotional, and mental tension and anxiety. As mindfulness helps you become more keenly aware of thought patterns that perhaps once served you but now hinder your growth, you can gain some distance from these ways of thinking and begin to relate to them differently, much like recognizing that a well-worn shirt doesn't suit you anymore.

And as you become alert to and interested in the flow and context of your thoughts, you can recognize their many flavors, colors, and intensities: worrying, predicting, judging, speculating, conceptualizing, planning, forming opinions, hypothesizing, expecting, assuming, ruminating, cogitating, reflecting, contemplating, and more. Some thoughts come with a high emotional charge, and this is often true of anxious thoughts. This can make it challenging to turn toward these thoughts with mindfulness. In difficult times, remember these key points:

- Thoughts are not in your control.
- Thoughts are influenced in part by your past experience.
- Thoughts are not necessarily the truth.

Bearing these facts in mind will help you apply self-compassion, patience, and nonjudgment in the face of difficult thoughts. These and all of the attitudes of mindfulness will stand you in good stead as you commit to paying attention to your patterns of thinking. Although this work is challenging, it's highly worthwhile, allowing you to change your relationship to your thoughts, gaining some distance from them and increasing your ability to work with them more skillfully.

Imagination and Anxiety

As discussed, fear is a mind-body reaction to a perceived threat in the present moment, whereas anxiety is a mind-body reaction to an imagined future threat—something that may never actually happen. In fact, the future seldom plays out as imagined—something you explored mindfully in chapter 3. Here's a story that illustrates this dynamic well.

A man who was driving along got a flat tire late one evening on a deserted country road. He had a spare tire, but part of his jack was missing. As the sky got darker, he realized he needed to take action and get help. Seeing a dim light in a house in the distance, he decided to walk to the house and ask if he might borrow a jack. As he walked toward the house, his mind was filled with negative thoughts: *Maybe no one even lives in that house, and even if people do live there, they may be frightened when a complete stranger approaches the door. And even if they aren't frightened, they may not have a jack. And even if they have a jack, they may not want to lend it to me. They may be very stingy or distrustful—the type of people who would never help someone else, even a poor guy who's stranded with a flat tire!* The thoughts just kept piling up, one on top of the next, solidifying how impossible, difficult, and unhelpful the people in that house might be. The man's anxiety increased and he started to get angry at how unhelpful these people might be. Finally, he reached the house and knocked, and an old woman opened the door. "Can I help you?" she asked. By this point, the man could only see his idea of the people living in that house, not the actual woman standing before him, and yelled, "Okay, if that's how you want to be, you can keep your damn jack!"

When you imagine outcomes that may never happen, you're engaging in a kind of predictive thinking. It's like holding a telescope that peers into the future but can't really focus clearly.

The Power of Paying Attention to Thinking

As mentioned, there's a common but unfortunate tendency to identify with thinking and buy into the content of thoughts, believing them to be unassailably true. When you apply mindfulness to seeing thoughts as thoughts, you can begin to form a whole new relationship with them in all of their flavors, including worries, predictions, judgments, and opinions. Mindfulness puts you in a more stable and grounded position to see these thoughts for what they are: a stream of anxious cognitions focused on the future and the worst possible outcome.

Still, learning to take this stance toward anxious thinking can be difficult, and it takes practice because the conditioning that makes us believe we are our thoughts can make them stick like Velcro! To get unstuck you need to start checking this out for yourself and practicing it regularly, just as you strengthen your body with regular exercise. The next informal practice is a good way to start doing this, creating more space between yourself and whatever anxious thoughts might be filling you with doubt and dread.

Informal Practice: Checking In with Thoughts in Mountain Pose

Here's a brief but effective practice you can use anytime you're beset by anxious thoughts—or anytime whatsoever. It hearkens back to the informal practice in the previous chapter in which you used mountain pose to check in with your body. Take the same stance as in that practice, sitting or standing straight with your feet firmly planted on the ground. Align your shoulders over your hips and, if standing, your hips over your feet. Feel your neck and head upright and in balance, and let your arms rest next to your torso. In either position, you're taking the steady stance of a mountain—rooted, balanced, and grounded yet elevated.

As you settle into this position, focus on your breath for a moment, then turn your awareness to your thoughts. Whether they are random wanderings, anxious predictions, or something else entirely, simply notice them and watch the way they come and go, passing like the clouds in the sky. You can be present for each thought, and also for the spaces between them. There's no need to take them too seriously. Just as a mountain remains strong, enduring, and present to the clouds, you can remain present, balanced, and awake to the flow of thoughts. You can practice just briefly, for a few moments, or you can extend the practice longer if you like.

Try pausing with this informal practice several times a day. The more frequently you pause and remain steady amidst the flow of thoughts, the more you'll establish new ways of relating to your thoughts.

Forming a New Relationship with Thinking

There are many different ways to shift your relationship with thinking. Here are three that we find helpful. All of them can refine your relationship to anxious thoughts and enhance your experience of living.

Attending to the Body

The content of thoughts, especially worried or anxious thoughts, tends to pull you away from the present, whereas awareness of physical sensations brings you home to your present-moment experience. Because physical sensations always occur right in the here and now, and nowhere else, the body is a safe harbor when tides of anxious thoughts come in. By attending to physical sensations, whether pleasant or unpleasant, such as feeling your feet on the ground or the air touching your skin; by opening to sounds or smells; and of course by always taking the support of the breath—you come home to the actual moment of being alive, and you will be less pulled into an imagined future or other contents of thoughts. And because sensations in the body can only be known in the present moment, each time you redirect your attention to the body you gather energy that you might otherwise be spending on what-ifs. From this grounded place, you can bring more creativity to bear on meeting challenges.

Making More Space

When you turn your attention to the space that holds thoughts, you shift from a narrow focus to a panoramic view. This is like the space above, below, and between the cars of the train of thought, or the space in the sky that holds passing clouds of thoughts. Without pushing or pulling, you can allow thoughts to simply be there, being aware of their presence but also seeing the larger space they exist within. Breathing into this practice can help you cultivate more ease. With this wider perspective, you can be present with thoughts without getting lost in them or stuck to them. Again, this creates more opportunities to make mindful choices that aren't dictated by habitual thought patterns.

Seeing Thoughts as Waves on the Ocean

Similar to seeing thoughts as clouds in the sky or cars of a train, you might consider anxious thoughts to simply be choppy waves on a very deep and vast ocean. The waves rise, crest, and fall, and throughout they are just one part of a much larger experience. The ocean is your being and awareness, whereas thoughts are passing waves. When you pause to experience thoughts as simply rising and falling like this, you hold them in the vast expanse of your entire being, and you know that no single thought, no matter how troubling, will endure for long.

Informal Practice: Offering Hospitality to Anxious Thoughts

One way to increase your skill in working with anxiety is to become familiar with the early signs that you're becoming anxious. This varies from person to person. For you, it might be tightness at the stomach or heat in the face, or it may be a vague sense of insecurity, nervousness, or dread. Identifying these early signs will greatly enhance your ability to intercede in the cascade of anxiety early, before it builds momentum. As you begin to create more balance and equilibrium in this way, it will be easier to see anxious thoughts as simply clouds of fantasy, rather than threatening thunderheads. From this perspective, you can see your thoughts as simply formations moving through the mind. Then, when you don't have to fight, deny, or escape these thoughts and the physical and emotional reactions they bring up, you can greet all of the experiences of your present moment and offer them deeper hospitality. That may sound a little vague, so here are some concrete steps to apply as you meet anxious thoughts:

1. Connect with the body as soon as you notice that you're being carried away on a stream of anxious thoughts. Bring attention to the breath and how your body contacts whatever surface you stand, sit, or rest upon. Open your eyes to the world around you. Listen mindfully to whatever sounds are available in the present moment. Fully invite yourself to the here and now.

2. Remember that thoughts are not truths; they're just thoughts. No matter how harsh a critical self-judgment is, it's just a judgment. No matter how dire an imagined outcome, that doesn't mean it will actually happen.

3. Take several deep, slow breaths.

4. Look objectively at the thoughts you're having and ask yourself whether they're accurate. What do you genuinely know in this situation?

5. Acknowledge, if possible, how these thoughts are trying to protect you by helping you be prepared for the future. Perhaps you might even thank your mind for its attempt, no matter how misguided, to protect you and keep you safe in the future.

6. Patiently remain present with physical sensations, expanding to sense your entire body. Stay with whole body awareness for a few full cycles of breath.

7. Offer kindness to yourself by embracing your fearful thoughts like a baby who needs tender care. Allow yourself to be just as you are, whole and complete in this moment.

Formal Practice: Mindful Standing Yoga

Building on the mindful floor yoga practice in chapter 4, here we offer mindful standing yoga to help you build your commitment and strength to live fully, meeting anxiety with skill, flexibility, and equanimity. Standing postures invite you to take a stand in your life, including when choosing to mindfully work with the pull of anxious thoughts. Taking some time during your day to move your body with mindful awareness can help you feel more courageous, balanced, and awake to your intention to live with greater ease and can also encourage calm and steadiness. All of the guidelines in chapter 4 apply here: practicing in a warm space, wearing comfortable clothing, attending to your breath and allowing it to flow freely, honoring your body's limits, and consulting with a health care provider if you have any questions about whether these movements are appropriate for you.

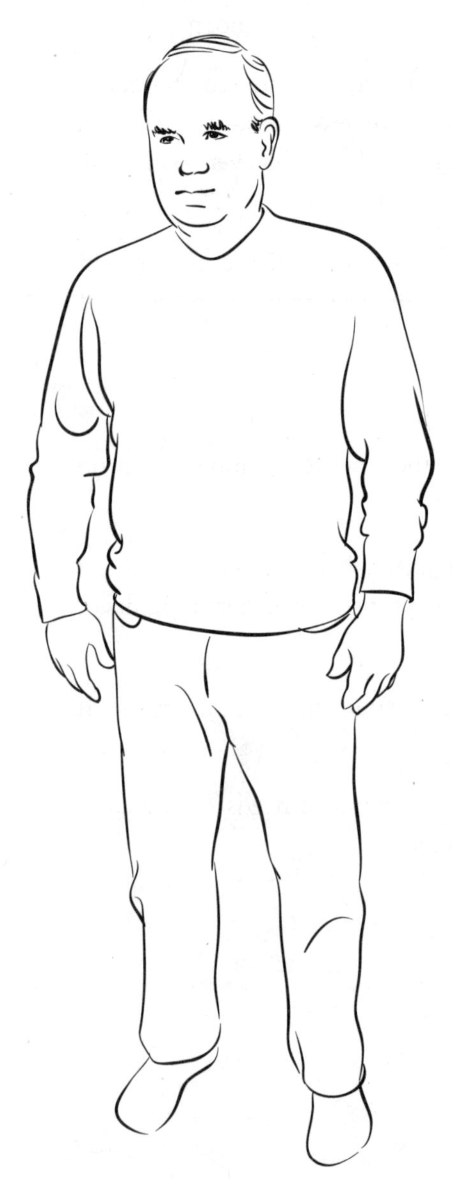

As mentioned in chapter 4, mindful yoga is most beneficial if you commit to regular, consistent practice. Once you've learned the poses below, the entire sequence can be done in fifteen to forty-five minutes. We've also provided downloadable audio instructions, available in three versions—fifteen, thirty, and forty-five minutes—at http://www.newharbinger.com/29736 (see the back of this book for instructions on how to access them). Please schedule a time to practice regularly, perhaps alternating with the sitting meditation practice you'll learn next.

Mountain Pose

Because we presented mountain pose in informal practices in chapter 4 and earlier in this chapter, it should be familiar to you at this point. In standing yoga, mountain pose plays a role similar to that of corpse pose in floor yoga, creating a stable foundation and serving as a place to return to between poses so the body can integrate the effects of other postures. So as you've previously practiced, stand with awareness. Feel your feet bearing your weight. Sense the upright quality of the torso while you stand tall, creating a sense of spaciousness. Allow your feet, shoulders, and jaw to receive the pull of gravity as you stand firmly rooted, stable, and grounded yet elevated. As you stand like a mountain, bring awareness to your entire body.

Shoulder Rolls

Standing tall in mountain pose, gently lift your shoulders toward your ears, then lower them. Next, bring them forward, toward the center of your chest, then move them backward, squeezing your shoulder blades together. Next, begin to bring these movements together, slowly and gently rolling your shoulders down, forward, up, and back. Allowing your breath to flow freely, stay with the sensations in your upper body as you circle your shoulders. After a few repetitions, reverse the direction, slowly rolling your shoulders down, back, up, and forward, allowing your breath to flow freely.

Head Turns

Standing tall in mountain pose, feel a sense of length in your neck, with the crown of your head reaching slightly upward. Maintaining this feeling of length and ease, slowly and gently twist your head to the right as far as you comfortably can, allowing your breath to flow freely. Return to center, then twist your head to the left in the same way. Repeat as many times as you like, moving slowly and fluidly. Return to mountain pose, then slowly and gently bend your neck forward, bringing your chin to your chest and allowing your breath to flow freely. Return to the neutral position, then gently bend your neck to the back, looking up and being sure to keep your neck long. Repeat as many times as you like, moving slowly and fluidly.

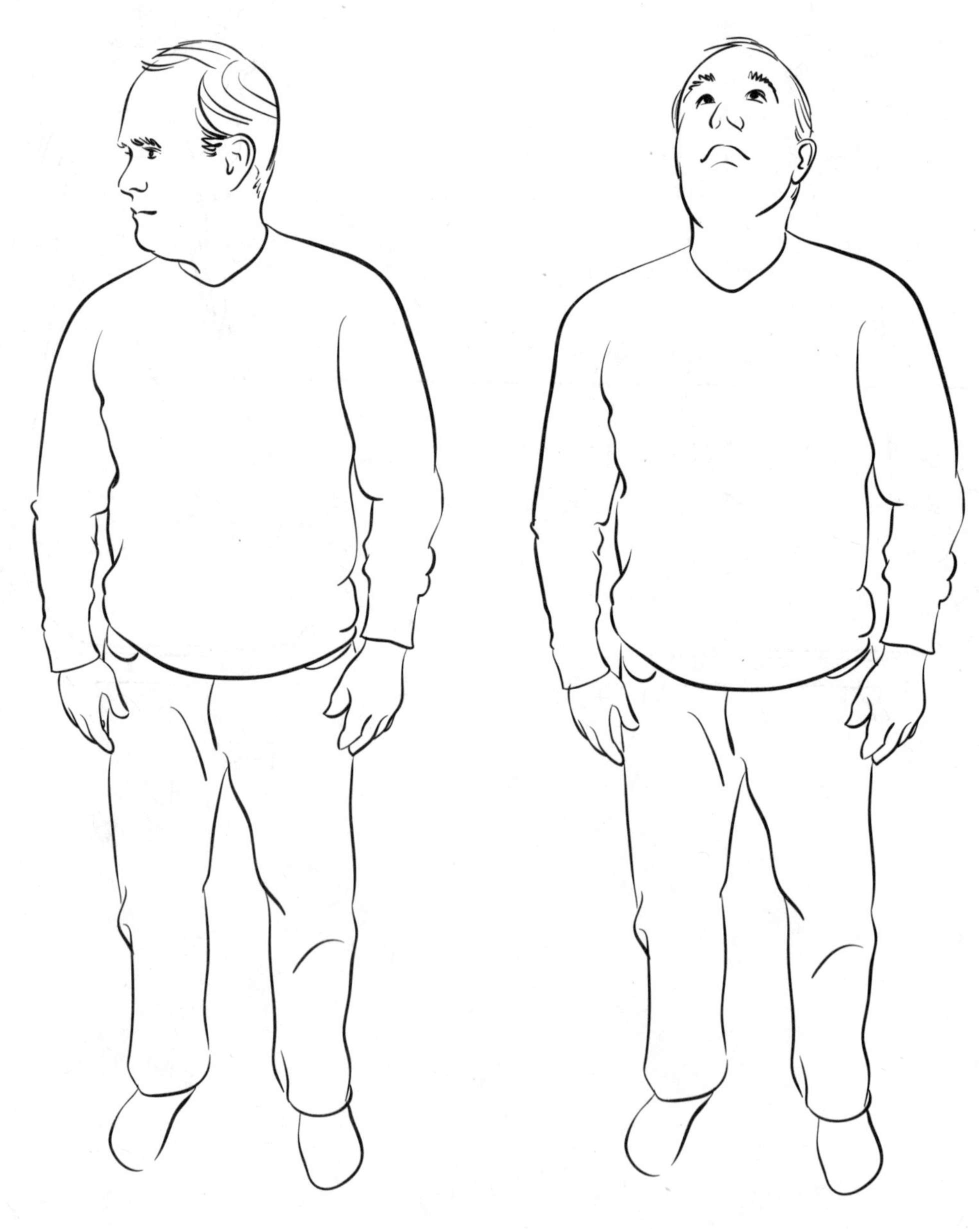

Standing Cat and Cow

For this standing version of cat and cow, place your feet to be about twelve inches apart. Bend your knees slightly and place hands on your thighs just above your knees, being careful not to put pressure on your knees. Breathe in deeply, then, as you exhale, bend your back, bringing your upper body forward, lowering your chin, and tightening your abdomen. This is the standing cat pose. Then, as you inhale, extend your buttocks and shoulders back while arching your waist forward and gently raising your chin. This is the standing cow pose. Moving with your breath, repeat the poses several times, then gently return to mountain pose.

Side Leg Lifts

For this pose, feel free to use a prop, such as a chair, to help you maintain your balance. As you stand in mountain pose, gently shift your weight to your right leg and begin to lift your left leg, extending it out to the side. If using a prop, try to touch it lightly, rather than gripping it. Maintain this balanced pose as long as you like, allowing your breath to flow freely and feeling how dynamic this stationary position is, with your body making numerous tiny adjustments to maintain balance. Gently return to mountain pose and rest there for a breath or two. Then repeat on the other side, shifting your weight to your left leg and extending your right leg out to the side, then returning to mountain pose.

Upward Stretch

This pose is similar to the long stretch in chapter 4, here being done in a standing position. Standing in mountain pose, gently raise your arms up toward the sky and stretch, keeping your spine vertical and breathing freely. Feel into the stretch along your sides and sense your feet firmly planted on the ground as you reach skyward. As you're ready, return to mountain pose.

Crescent

From mountain pose, repeat the upward stretch, and while in the stretched position, turn your palms toward each other and gently bend from your waist toward the left, keeping your spine long. Stretch as far as is challenging without straining, and breathe freely. Slowly return to center, then repeat on the other side. To deepen the stretch, when bending to the left hold your right wrist in your left hand, and vice versa.

Warrior Pose

Practicing the warrior pose can encourage you to remember your vision, intention, and strength. To begin, stand in mountain pose, balanced and upright, with your hips over your feet, your shoulders over your hips, your arms at your sides, and your neck and head balanced. Bring awareness to being grounded and tall. Widen your stance so your feet are two or three feet apart. Turn your left foot 90 degrees to the left. Sensing into the contact between your feet and the floor and the strength in your legs, extend your arms out to the sides in a T shape and bend your left knee, bringing it over your ankle and no farther. Keep your midline, from your tailbone to the crown of your head, vertical. Turn your head to the left and gaze out over your left hand, breathing freely. You should be able to see your toes as you maintain the alignment of your knee over your ankle. Feel into this posture, which is grounded, strong, open, and focused. All of these qualities are within you.

To come out of this posture, turn your left foot forward, parallel to your right foot, lower your arms, and turn your head forward. Then repeat on the other side, turning your right foot 90 degrees to the right. Bend your right knee, aligning your knee over your ankle. Extend your arms to the sides and turn your head to the right, gazing over your right hand. As you come out of this posture, align your feet and head straight forward and lower your arms to your sides. Establish your mountain pose and mindfully check in with how you're feeling.

Mindful Journaling

Right after your first practice of mindful standing yoga, take a few moments to write about your experience. How did it go for you? What did you notice in your body, mind, and emotions? And how are you feeling right now?

____

____

____

____

____

____

Formal Practice: Sitting Meditation

In your formal practice of mindful breathing, you've already begun to practice sitting meditation, maintaining a strong focus on the breath. For this practice, you'll begin with mindful breathing and then shift to different objects of attention: first the entire body (as practiced in chapter 3), then progressing through sounds, thoughts, and emotions, and ultimately transitioning to choiceless awareness, in which you rest awareness broadly and notice whatever is most prominent in the moment. In this way, you'll practice collecting your attention on one point or object and then widening to a more spacious awareness in which you don't choose any particular object of intention but instead are present with whatever rises in the field of awareness in each unfolding moment. Through this practice, you have the opportunity to develop attention by returning again and again to the present each time the mind wanders from a particular focus, and also to rest in awareness with the constant coming and going of thoughts, emotions, and sensations without choosing one particular focus.

If you haven't done so already, you may wish to establish a place and time for formal meditation practice that best suits your lifestyle. Offering yourself the time to be fully with yourself and care for yourself by bringing curiosity to your inner and outer experience, moment to moment, is a powerful way to cultivate the steadiness, presence, and patience that will help you meet anxious times with grace and skill.

The instructions below are for a seated posture. But as always, please attend to your particular needs. If sitting isn't appropriate for your body now, it's fine to stand or lie down as described in chapter 2. (If lying down, it may be especially important to invite an attitude of alertness.) So that you can fully experience this meditation without referring to the book, we recommend that you listen to the downloadable audio instructions, which are available in three versions—fifteen, thirty, and forty-five minutes—at http://www.newharbinger.com/29736. However, you can also simply read the text below. If you choose to read, read through the entire script first to familiarize yourself with the practice, then do the meditation, referring back to the text as needed and pausing briefly after each paragraph. Initially, take about fifteen minutes for the practice. With time, you can extend the duration.

Begin by establishing your posture, sitting steady and upright, balanced and grounded, either in a chair or on a cushion. You can gently close your eyes or just lower your gaze toward the floor. Place your hands in your lap or on your thighs in a way that's relatively comfortable. Your attitude and posture are an expression of your dignity and your willingness to bring attention and interest to your life, moment to moment. By bringing mindfulness to each passing moment and sensing into your body's experience, you can meet whatever you encounter with skill and wisdom. If you find that you're experiencing pain at any point in this meditation, pause with the reactive impulse to escape the sensation, and then pause for a moment longer to explore the sensations that make your experience unpleasant. Based on this patient investigation, slowly shift your position to one with greater ease. In this way, you practice mindfully engaging with your experience and responding rather than reacting to unpleasantness.

Having established your position, bring attention to your breathing. Rest with the breath as it moves into and out of your body. Where do you feel this most vividly? At the nostrils or in the throat? Perhaps in the touch of air on your upper lip? With each breath, perhaps you feel your chest expand and then return to center. Or maybe you sense movement in your belly, rising and falling, or a deeper, more subtle movement of the breath in your abdomen. Whichever place feels most available to you, rest your awareness within those sensations. The sensations may be strong or subtle. Either is fine. What's most important is the quality you bring to attending in each moment.

When you discover that the mind has wandered away from the sensations of breathing, firmly yet gently return to the felt sense of the next breath. Training your attention takes time, repetition, and patience. But remember, each time you discover that you're lost in thought, you're actually awake again. So, with curiosity, just redirect your attention to a single, pointed focus on the breath when you find that you aren't in the moment. Does this next breath feel shallow, deep, long, or short? By being present breath by breath and escorting your attention back to the object of attention time and time again, you're cultivating a steady, easy approach to working with your mind.

Now begin to widen your focus from sensations of the breath to the entire body. As your focus broadens to the whole body, you may notice a variety of sensations, from the level of your skin to deep within you. You may be aware of a vibrant and changing field of sensations that rise from within, perhaps in the form of pulsing, throbbing, expanding, contracting, warmth, or coolness. Notice the feelings of pressure and contact with the surface that supports you and the sensations inherent in the position you're in. Perhaps you'll find awareness of sensations in the mouth: dryness, moisture, or a taste. Maybe you'll feel sensations on your skin or sense the shift of light and shadow on your eyes. Perhaps you'll perceive scents and sounds. Some parts of the body may feel numb or seem to have no strong sensations at all. Just be with whatever you experience internally and externally in the body… being with what is here now and feeling these sensations come and go.

As you open to the entire body as a field of sensation, you may discover sensations that are pleasant, unpleasant, or neutral. You may find some unpleasant sensations to be painful or distressing. As you've learned in practicing the body scan, you have a number of options for working with pain. You can pause and bring curiosity to the sensation. Is it hot, burning, pulling, or tingling?

With attentiveness, you can move closer to and into the experience. With intention, you can choose to move away and redirect your focus to the breath...moving toward and away, touching into the discomfort gently, and intentionally redirecting your focus. You can also hold painful sensations in the larger container of the whole body.

Now allow the breath and whole body to move toward the background and begin to focus on hearing...being present with each unfolding moment of sound. There's no need to name the source of the sound. Just stay receptive to and aware of these vibrations that travel through the air to your ears, perhaps noticing loudness, softness, closeness, or distance, or the suddenness or continuity of sounds as they come and go. Whenever your mind wanders, gently escort it back to whatever sounds are present, internal or external.

Now allow sound and hearing to recede to the background and turn your attention to thoughts and thinking. As you do this, you may initially find it quite challenging to be present with thoughts without getting lost in them. This is natural and common; people often identify with their thoughts, seeing their thoughts as being who they are. When you become aware that you've fallen into the content of a thought, you can redirect your attention to a more panoramic view of thoughts coming and going, moving in the space of the mind like clouds in the vast blue sky, seeing awareness as an immense expanse that thinking emerges from. Stay present to thoughts as they form and fade away. Some may be familiar, some sticky, and some random surprises. Allow them all to come and go as you remain steady in your posture and presence.

Now turn your focus to emotions. They can be very close to thoughts, and also very close to the body, often being felt in sensations in the body. As best you can, turn your attention to whatever streams of emotion may be present. Some may be strong and gripping, others barely apparent. There's no need to search for emotions. Just remain steadfast in your attention, with curiosity, as these streams emerge, endure for a while, and then move on.

Now release emotions and any other particular object of awareness and be present with whatever arises in this unfolding moment of experience, resting in choiceless awareness. As your experience continually shifts, you may be aware of thinking, then a sensation, then an emotion, then your entire body, then a sound, and so on. Stay mindfully aware of whatever is prominent and distinct as you open to your changing experience. If at any time this feels too broad or overwhelming, you can steady your practice by focusing on the breath or whole body. Then, as you feel ready, shift again to the choiceless choice of being with whatever arises in your dynamic experience of your body and mind in the moment. While remaining open in this way, you may become aware of a sense of silence and stillness. Whatever your experience, just rest with being open to the moment as it emerges.

Now return to the breath, feeling the ongoing cycle of inhalation and exhalation and the body responding with each breath. Take a deeper breath and release it with a long, slow exhalation. Then, as you're ready, open your eyes and gently stretch in any way that feels right in the moment. As you bring this practice to a close, take a few moments to acknowledge your willingness to engage with your life and experience so directly. You've turned toward your body and mind with interest and curiosity, and you're cultivating your ability to remain present to your ever-changing experience in life, including moments of anxiety.

Mindful Journaling

Right after your first practice of sitting meditation, take a few moments to write about your experience. How did it go for you? What did you notice in your body, mind, and emotions? And how are you feeling right now?

____

____

____

____

____

____

Planning Your Formal Practice

In this chapter you learned two new formal practices: mindful standing yoga and sitting meditation. Please practice them daily for the next week, perhaps alternating which one you practice from day to day. It's fine to add any of the previous practices as well, but for the next week, be sure to practice those in this chapter. As usual, we recommend scheduling your practice times in advance and making a commitment to keep these appointments with yourself. Then, use the following form to note each time you practice and briefly describe your experience (for a downloadable version, visit http://www.newharbinger.com/29736).

Mindful Standing Yoga and Sitting Meditation Practice Log

Day and time: ____

Your experience: ____

____

Day and time: ______________________

Your experience: ______________________

____

Day and time: ______________________

Your experience: ______________________

____

Day and time: ______________________

Your experience: ______________________

____

Day and time: ______________________

Your experience: ______________________

____

Day and time: ______________________

Your experience: ______________________

____

Day and time: ______________________

Your experience: ______________________

____

Closing the Chapter

In this chapter you explored the nature of thoughts and ways to form a new relationship with thinking through the practice of mindfulness—in particular, seeing that you have thoughts but are much more than your thinking. You learned that thoughts play a big role in the experience of anxiety, and you explored ways to meet anxious thoughts with equanimity—as a mountain experiences the clouds, as the ocean encompasses waves—specifically by grounding yourself in the present moment through turning your attention to your body. You also practiced mindful standing yoga and a sitting meditation that incorporates choiceless awareness. In all of these ways, you're building your skill in experiencing the fullness of who you are.

In the next chapter, we'll turn to mindfulness practice with a focus on how to engage with anxious emotions. Your deepening connection with your body and increasing nimbleness in your relationship with your thoughts will form a strong foundation as you investigate your experience with anxious emotions more deeply. To help you gather your courage for this challenging but rewarding and highly worthwhile work, consider this poem by Danna Faulds (2002, 25; reprinted with permission), which invites us to let go and be free.

Allow

There is no controlling life.
Try corralling a lightning bolt,
containing a tornado. Dam a
stream and it will create a new
channel. Resist, and the tide
will sweep you off your feet.
Allow, and grace will carry
you to higher ground. The only
safety lies in letting it all in—
the wild and the weak; fear,
fantasies, failures and success.
When loss rips off the doors of
the heart, or sadness veils your
vision with despair, practice
becomes simply bearing the truth.
In the choice to let go of your
known way of being, the whole
world is revealed to your new eyes.

Chapter 6

A Mindful Way of Meeting Anxious Emotions

In the previous two chapters you learned about how anxiety affects your body and your thoughts, and began to engage in mindfulness practices that can play a strategic role in diminishing anxious states in both body and mind. In this chapter we'll look at how mindfulness practice can work with and transform anxiety-related emotions, including panic, fear, excessive worry, concern, irritation, nervousness, angst, jitteriness, irritability, exasperation, and feeling overwhelmed.

When you feel the rush of anxiety racing through your body and the worrying thoughts it generates, you're likely to feel a range of emotions as well—not just fear, but possibly also anger, confusion, grief, embarrassment, shame, or sadness. The emotions associated with anxiety are typically difficult to be with and endure because they feel so uncomfortable. Sometimes you may even feel like you're crawling out of your own skin. These emotions often create patterns of reactivity that may become habitual and prevent you from living fully. These conditioned reactions can color your experience, distort your interpretation of events, and feed into a cycle of anxiety. Mindfulness can help diminish those reactive patterns by allowing you to recognize that you have a choice about how to respond to anxiety. You can begin to respond constructively rather than reacting habitually and perhaps destructively.

In addition, when you experience emotions that feel unpleasant and negative, this is likely to create or add to a sense of discouragement and disheartenment. So you may wish to, or even try to, push these emotions away. However, emotions aren't something we can control. What you can do is recognize how emotions affect your overall state, which is the first step toward being less enslaved by them.

Turning Toward Anxious Emotions

Based on what you've learned in previous chapters, you probably have a good idea of where we'll be going in this chapter. We'll be asking you to turn toward anxious emotions (and other kinds) with mindful awareness. You may be thinking, *Why would I want to bring mindfulness to my anxious emotions? What I really want is to get rid of them!* This is understandable. And in fact, though it may seem paradoxical, turning mindful attention to anxious emotions can help ease anxiety.

From our point of view, the best way to work with anxious emotions is to mindfully acknowledge them and bring greater understanding to what's fueling anxiety so you can gradually begin to transform challenging emotions or your relationship to them. Developing this understanding involves looking into and investigating old patterns of conditioning that you've accumulated over your lifetime. Human beings are creatures of habit, and many of us begin building habitual patterns of behaving and reacting early in our lives, influenced by various life situations. For example, if you were brought up in an environment that wasn't safe, you may have become guarded and fearful. If you were shamed, you may feel inadequate and socially inept. If you were told you'd never amount to anything, you might feel fearful and deficient. All of these feelings can clearly play a role in anxiety. There are many factors involved in why you feel the way you do and how you perceive the world.

The task before you is to become more aware of how you see the world and yourself, through your body, thoughts, and emotions. These aspects of yourself are the laboratory you bring mindfulness to. Although the work of turning your attention to anxious emotions and habitual reactions can be quite challenging at times, through this approach you may come to realize that the way you've been living your life isn't serving you well, opening the door to the possibility of change and greater freedom.

From a mindfulness perspective, working with your emotions and learning to regulate them is paramount for experiencing balance and comfort within your body and mind. As you create more peace within yourself emotionally, quite naturally your body and mind will begin to feel more at ease. The key is to create a gap in the vicious cycle of anxiety—a space between whatever triggers your anxiety and your reaction to that trigger. This is the opening you need to move through and beyond anxiety. As you become familiar with that space, you'll discover that there's more to your experience than you may have realized, including many positive feelings that can more than balance the overbearing, negative emotions of anxiety that tend to be the focus of attention. Likewise, by becoming familiar with the full range of your emotions and acknowledging them, you can see that any given emotion is not the totality of who you are.

Informal Practice: Pause, Inquire, Acknowledge

This informal practice will help you become familiar with that all-important gap between a challenging event and your reaction. It's a powerful yet simple way to cool the rush of anxious emotions that may come up in your daily life, and an approach that you can bring to any difficult situation. There are three steps to this informal practice: pausing, inquiring, and acknowledging.

1. **Pause.** When you feel the surge of an anxious emotion and feel an impulse to react, try to pause for a moment and become mindful of your breath. This is the crucial space between the stimulus and the reaction. By pausing, you transform it into a moment of repose.

2. **Inquire.** Investigate your direct experience of anxiety in your body and mind. Bring curiosity to the experience and all of its sensory aspects. Also notice any thoughts, as well as any emotions that may have been evoked by your anxiety. This fosters openness to learning about what's driving your anxiety and how it affects you. By helping you see more clearly, such inquiry increases your self-knowledge and wisdom.

3. **Acknowledge.** The last step is to acknowledge whatever you're experiencing: fear, angst, upset, anger, muscle tension, heart palpitations, sweating—anything and everything that arises in the mind and body. If this feels difficult, imagine yourself as a vast ocean, with plenty of room for these waves of experience to rise and fall. As you acknowledge all of the experiences evoked by anxiety and allow them to go wherever they need to go, they will gradually dissipate.

Colleen's Story

Colleen lived with social anxiety on nearly a daily basis. At work she was quite competent, performing well in meetings and displaying excellent interpersonal communication skills, but when it came to social situations she became nervous and uncomfortable because of old fears of not being accepted and liked.

Colleen isolated herself during her lunch hour, and she dreaded Christmas parties and other work-related social events. She usually came up with excuses not to go, but sometimes she ended up attending. When she did, she desperately attempted to keep the conversations focused on work. Yet even this approach didn't serve her well, as it left her feeling uncomfortable and shallow. She could see how others were enjoying themselves and envied them. She wished she could be like them, but she felt so stuck in her ways of relating to others. Her behavior had become very limiting, and she felt imprisoned by it.

When Colleen heard about mindfulness meditation and its many benefits, she wondered if it might be helpful for her. She started reading up on it. Then a friend told her about a mindfulness class, and Colleen decided to take a leap and enroll in it, even though she was terrified by the prospect of being with strangers in an unknown situation. But at the same time, she also felt that her life was becoming increasingly constricted. She had few friends and almost no social life. She didn't want to live with social anxiety for the rest of her life.

In the early sessions of the mindfulness class, Colleen learned practices of mindful breathing and sitting meditation, and she was pleased to discover that continued practice helped decrease her anxiety. But what she found most helpful was the informal practice of pausing, inquiring, and acknowledging, which allowed her to bring mindfulness into social situations and transform her anxiety.

When the time came for the annual picnic at the company where Colleen worked, she felt a lot of apprehension, but she was also eager to attend and have some fun with her colleagues. Before she left home for the picnic, she practiced mindful breathing for a few minutes, until she felt centered and relaxed.

After driving to the picnic, Colleen parked and took a few mindful breaths to settle down. Sitting there in her car, she found herself flooded with anxiety and wished she could just be at home. Recognizing the familiar experience of anxiety arising once again, she decided to use the informal practice of pausing, inquiring, and acknowledging.

When she paused, she could sense the entire cascade of reactivity arising within her, but rather than jumping aboard that train, she took a few moments to mindfully breathe in and out. Then she inquired into her direct experience, noting what she felt in her body and mind. She felt her heart racing and her palms sweating, noticed strong emotions of apprehension and embarrassment, and realized that she was thinking It's never going to stop. *Then she acknowledged all of the sensations, thoughts, and emotions she observed and just let them be, giving them some space until the intensity began to subside.*

Joyfully, Colleen recognized that she was mindfully responding to the anxiety rather than mindlessly reacting to it. This understanding gave her a sense of equanimity and balance, and from her new perspective, she knew the anxiety wouldn't last forever. This allowed her to see that the limiting story she'd told herself again and again, about being a failure socially, didn't serve her well.

As she stepped out of her car, Colleen felt a new sense of confidence. She realized that she was neither more nor less than anyone else at the picnic, and that she had something unique to offer. She also recalled something her mother had shared years ago, saying that the secret of making friends is to ask personal questions and to listen to people's replies deeply, from your heart. Her mom said most people love to talk about themselves, and if you listen kindly, they're likely to want to know more about you too.

As Colleen approached the gathering, she saw her coworker Sam and asked him how he was doing. Sam seemed to be taken aback, probably because he was shocked to see Colleen being so forthright and friendly, then responded that he was great, and it was nice to see her. Colleen paused briefly as she internally acknowledged a twinge of awkwardness, then told Sam that it was nice to see him too. Emboldened, she then inquired about how Sam's knee was healing from a skiing injury. Sam was so touched that he started rattling on about how he was doing and then cracked a joke. They both started laughing, and Colleen realized that she felt at ease and was even enjoying herself. Her success in her conversation with Sam gave her confidence to talk with others, and before the afternoon was over, she'd had many meaningful conversations and shared laughter with quite a few people. As she drove home, she felt as though a new day had dawned, and she was excited about the next chapter in her life.

Walking Meditation

In chapters 4 and 5 we introduced formal practices of lying and standing yoga. Here, we'll look at another form of mindful movement: walking meditation. Walking meditation is an immediate and natural pathway to tuning in to the body and becoming more grounded. In day-to-day life, walking is generally associated with getting somewhere—traveling from point A to B. Walking meditation is all point A or, more accurately, each point along the way. With every step you arrive in the present moment. In the word of Zen master Thich Nhat Hahn, "The miracle is not to walk on water. The miracle is to walk on the green earth in the present moment, to appreciate the peace and beauty that are available now" (1992, 1).

There are two types of walking meditation: narrow gauge and wide gauge. In this chapter you'll learn the narrow-gauge practice, in which your attention is akin to a laser beam, focusing awareness tightly on each aspect of walking. Later, in chapter 10, we'll introduce you to the wide-gauge practice, in which your attention is more like a floodlight, connecting you with the surrounding environment as you take each step.

Formal Practice: Narrow-Gauge Walking Meditation

In narrow-gauge mindful walking, you bring attention to the intricate movements involved in walking, which tend to occur automatically and beneath the level of conscious awareness: shifting of your body weight onto one foot and leg, lifting the other foot, moving it forward, placing it down, and shifting your weight onto that foot and leg. This type of walking can be done over a very short distance, perhaps ten to fifteen feet, as you mindfully walk from one point to the other and then turn around and walk back to where you started.

To allow you to fully experience this meditation without referring to the book, we recommend that you listen to the downloadable audio version, which is available at http://www.newharbinger.com/29736 (see the back of this book for instructions on how to access it). However, you can also simply read the text below. If you do, read through the entire script first to familiarize yourself with the practice, then do the practice, referring back to the text as needed and pausing briefly after each paragraph. Initially, take five to fifteen minutes for the practice. With time, you can extend the duration.

Mindfully stand, feeling your feet on the floor or ground and your connection to the earth below.

Gently shift your weight to your left foot, leg, and hip and begin to lift your right foot. With attention and intention, move your right foot forward, then place it on the ground.

Move at a pace that allows you to maintain your balance and awareness. Walking meditation can be done slowly, quickly, or at any pace between. Mindfulness is measured by awareness, not speed.

Now gently shift your weight onto your right foot, leg, and hip and begin to lift your left foot. With awareness of all of the sensations that arise, move your left foot forward, then place it on the ground.

Continue in this way, walking forward about ten feet, then turn around mindfully, attending to all of the sensations of turning. Then walk back to your starting point.

Throughout this practice, if you notice that your mind wanders, acknowledge wherever your mind went, then bring it back to walking: shifting your weight, then lifting, moving, and placing your foot.

Continue walking back and forth in this way for five to fifteen minutes, feeling your connection to the ground and being present.

As you're ready to finish this practice, take a moment to acknowledge yourself for devoting this time to yourself and mindfulness, nurturing your well-being and sense of ease and connection.

Mindful Journaling

Right after your first practice of narrow-gauge walking, take a few moments to write about your experience. How did it feel to walk mindfully, paying attention to each movement? What did you notice in your body, mind, and emotions? And how are you feeling right now?

____

____

____

____

____

____

TRY THIS!

One of the few constants in life is change. This is trustworthy. The inevitable force of impermanence is something all living beings experience. At times we desire or even relish change, and at times we resist it. While this unpredictability may feel insecure, embracing change as a fact of life can support innovation, creativity, and greater ease. Bringing curiosity to what unfolds in each passing moment can enliven your experience. Not knowing what will come next can allow for wonder and amazement, not just anxiety. You can build curiosity and acceptance slowly, starting with small experiences and gradually extending to others. Here are a few practices that can help you deepen your sense of wonder and befriend unexpected experiences.

- When you have a social engagement, explore not knowing what will happen, such as what your friends will order or make for dinner, what they'll talk about, what the physical environment will be like, and what emotions you might feel. Consider writing down some of your ideas about what might happen and then checking them out later. Allow this to be playful.
- You can hold even ambiguity and vulnerability with affectionate awareness. When you find yourself feeling anxious or frightened about what may happen, imagine holding these emotions and the related thoughts with gentle acceptance.
- When you notice yourself predicting how things will be in the future or how you'll feel now, imagine holding your prediction like a delicate, fragile bubble in the palm of your hand. Like a bubble, this thought about the future will change as you stay curious.

Bringing a sense of humor to these experiments will be helpful. Noticing the many predictions we make about how life will be and comparing them with what actually happens can help you take a more lighthearted attitude toward the way the mind works. It also can strengthen your self-compassion.

Formal Practice: Meditation on Anxious Emotions

Now we'll introduce a formal practice for working with anxious emotions. While it's similar to the informal practice of pausing, inquiring, and acknowledging, it involves deeper investigation into the causes of anxious feelings. Through this practice, you can discover the story lines that tend to trigger and drive your emotions. Although it may sometimes feel as though your anxiety comes out of nowhere, it usually has a source—typically some combination of conditioning, self-stories, memories, thoughts, and buried emotions.

That said, when you practice this meditation, don't try to force yourself to find the source or meaning of your anxiety. The crucial aspect of this meditation is to move forward in your journey of discovery into your self. Whatever you may find inside, simply acknowledging it will help you live with more ease. Then, rather than putting so much energy into fighting your anxiety, you can begin to change your relationship to it.

Because this practice involves intentionally exploring the experience of anxiety, it can be challenging. Before you do this practice, please take a little time to consider whether you're feeling up to it, listening to your inner voice to determine whether it feels right for you at this time. Consider doing your first practice when you feel safe and curious and have the energy and time to explore your anxiety more deeply. If now is not the time, be sure to return to this practice later, when you feel willing to take it on.

To allow you to fully experience this meditation without referring to the book, we recommend that you listen to the downloadable audio version, which is available at http://www.newharbinger.com/29736. However, you can also simply read the text below. If so, read through the entire script first to familiarize yourself with the practice, then do the practice, referring back to the text as needed and pausing briefly after each paragraph. Take about twenty minutes for the practice. You can do this practice in a seated position, standing, or even lying down. Choose a position in which you can be comfortable and alert.

> *Begin with a brief mindful check-in, taking a few minutes to acknowledge how you're currently feeling in your body and mind…being mindful of whatever is in your awareness and letting it all be. There's nothing that needs to be fixed, analyzed, or solved. Just allow your experience and let it be. Being present.*
>
> *Now gently shift your attention to the breath, becoming mindful of breathing in and out. Bring awareness to wherever you feel the breath most prominently and distinctly, perhaps at your nose, in your chest, or in your belly, or perhaps somewhere else. There's no other place you need to go… nothing else you need to do…just being mindful of your breath flowing in and out. If your mind wanders away from the breath, just acknowledge wherever it went, then return to being mindful of breathing in and out.*
>
> *Now reflect on a specific experience of anxiety, perhaps something recent so you can remember it more clearly. It doesn't have to be an extreme experience of anxiety, perhaps something that you'd rate at 5 or 6 on a scale of 1 to 10. Recall the experience in detail, as vividly as you can, invoking some of that anxiety now, in the present moment.*
>
> *As you imagine the experience and sense into it, be mindful of how the anxiety feels in your body and stay present with the sensations. Your only job right now is to feel and acknowledge whatever physical sensations you're experiencing in your body and let them be. There's no need to change them. Let the sensations run their course, just like a ripple on a lake is gradually assimilated into the entirety of the body of water.*
>
> *Now feel into any emotions that emerge…anxiety, fear, sadness, anger, confusion…whatever you may feel. As with physical sensations, just acknowledge how these emotions feel and let them be. There's no need to analyze them or figure them out.*

If strong emotions don't arise, this doesn't mean you aren't doing this meditation correctly. The practice is simply to acknowledge whatever is in your direct experience and let it be. Whatever comes up in the practice is the practice.

Bringing awareness to your anxiety may sometimes amplify your anxious feelings. This is normal, and the intensity will subside as you open to and acknowledge what you're experiencing and give it space to simply be.

Continue feeling into the anxiety, just allowing any feelings in the body and mind and letting them be, cultivating balance and the fortitude to be with things as they are. The very fact that you're acknowledging anxiety rather than turning away from it is healing.

As you continue to acknowledge your physical sensations and emotions, they may begin to reveal a host of memories, thoughts, feelings, and physical experiences that may have created limiting definitions of who you think you are. You may begin to see more clearly into how these old patterns of conditioning have driven your anxiety. This understanding can set you free—freer than you ever felt possible.

Now gradually transition back to the breath, breathing mindfully in and out… Next, slowly shift your awareness from your breath to sensing into your heart. Take some time to open into your heart with self-compassion, acknowledging your courage in engaging with your anxiety. In this way, your anxiety can become your teacher, helping you open your heart to greater wisdom, compassion, and ease within your being.

As you're ready to end this meditation, congratulate yourself for taking this time to meditate and heal yourself. Then gradually open your eyes and return to being present in the environment around you. May we all find the gateways into our hearts and be free.

Mindful Journaling

Right after your first practice of this meditation, take a few moments to write about your experience. How did it go for you? How did you work with what came up within your body, thoughts, and emotions? And how are you feeling right now?

____

____

____

____

____

____

Joseph's Story

Joseph's childhood seemed normal enough. He participated in sports, had many friends, and did well in school, although he sometimes felt uncomfortable when he had to stand up in class to answer a question or give a report. On occasion, after he answered a question incorrectly or flubbed a report, some of the other kids made so much fun of him that he felt deeply ashamed. After this happened a few times, he began to lose confidence in himself and tried to avoid speaking up in class.

In college, Joseph studied astronomy and excelled, yet he still tended to feel guarded and anxious when he had to speak in front of others. But because his early childhood experiences of being humiliated were long forgotten, he didn't understand why he got so anxious. He aspired to work at a planetarium, where he could share the marvels and mysteries of the universe with others, but didn't know how he could pursue this course when he dreaded the idea of public speaking.

Having heard that MBSR was an effective approach for easing anxiety, Joseph signed up for a class. He enjoyed the practices in the early sessions, but when the teacher began to introduce a meditation on anxious emotions, he felt a sense of dread. As the class practiced together, he held himself back, fearful of looking closely at his anxiety. After class, he explained his difficulty to his teacher. She encouraged him to give it another go and offered to guide him through the practice one-on-one. Reluctant but motivated at the same time, he agreed.

His teacher began by inviting Joseph to reflect on speaking in public and asked him to recall a specific experience. He brought to mind a recent presentation he'd given in class, and as he imagined it, he felt his forehead tightening, a pang in his chest, and a tightening in his gut. He also noticed that his breathing became irregular and rapid.

As Joseph felt into these physical sensations, his teacher invited him to acknowledge them and let them be. In time, some old memories from elementary school began to resurface. Seemingly out of nowhere, he remembered one kid making fun of him in math class when he answered a question incorrectly, and another kid making fun of him in history class when he stumbled over his words while giving a report. Then he remembered something else: after those painful incidents, he'd felt such immense shame that he vowed to never put himself in a vulnerable position again. As Joseph recalled those painful memories and feelings and acknowledged them, he finally understood what drove his anxiety: fear of being shamed and humiliated.

After the meditation, Joseph realized that his new understanding of what fueled his anxiety made him feel hopeful. He could see how his past conditioning fed into his anxiety and recognized that those past experiences didn't have to dictate his behavior now. This created an exciting sense of new possibilities and independence, in which he could free himself from his past conditioning.

Planning Your Formal Practice

In this chapter, you learned two new formal practices: narrow-gauge walking meditation and meditation on anxious emotions. We recommend that you do the mindful walking practice for at least fifteen minutes each day. In regard to meditation on anxious emotions, you can make that a daily practice or just do it whenever it feels right for you. Over the next week, on days when you don't do the meditation on anxious emotions, we recommend doing a different formal meditation, such as mindful breathing, the body scan, or sitting meditation. Use the following form to note each time you practice and briefly describe your experience. (For a downloadable version of it, visit http://www.newharbinger.com/29736).

Narrow-Gauge Walking and Meditation on Anxious Emotions Practice Log

Day and time: ____

Your experience: ____

____

Day and time: ____

Your experience: ____

____

Day and time: ____

Your experience: ____

____

Day and time: ____

Your experience: ____

____

Day and time: ____

Your experience: ____

____

Day and time: ____

Your experience: ____

____

Day and time: ____

Your experience: ____

____

Closing the Chapter

In this chapter, you learned both informal and formal practices for working with anxiety: the informal practice of pausing, inquiring, and acknowledging, and a formal meditation on anxious emotions. Engaging in these practices regularly will affirm your deep intention to bring mindfulness into your life to free yourself from anxiety. You also learned a formal walking meditation—yet another approach to grounding yourself in your body and the present moment as a way of working with anxious emotions.

In the next chapter, we'll look at bringing mindfulness to communication, both with others and within yourself, in the form of self-talk. What we say to ourselves and others can have a profound effect on anxiety, so it's well worth exploring in detail. But before you read on, take some time to reflect upon the following poem by Jennifer Welwood (1998, 21; reprinted with permission). It offers an eloquent description of willingness to turn toward fears and find your heart.

Unconditional

Willing to experience aloneness,
I discover connection everywhere;
Turning to face my fear,
I meet the warrior who lives within;
Opening to my loss,
I gain the embrace of the universe;
Surrendering into emptiness,
I find fullness without end.
Each condition I flee from pursues me,
Each condition I welcome transforms me
And becomes itself transformed
Into its radiant jewel-like essence.
I bow to the one who has made it so,
Who has crafted this Master Game;
To play it is purest delight—
To honor its form—true devotion.

Chapter 7

Mindful Communication

Communication is a dynamic exchange between your inner and outer experience that has a profound impact on whether you feel safe and at ease or anxious and threatened in your day-to-day life. Throughout this chapter, you'll continue to build and deepen your practice of mindfulness while beginning to turn toward the choice to be nonjudgmentally present, with interest, curiosity, and kindness, in your interactions with other people. In this way, you'll expand the scope of your mindfulness practice to the interpersonal contact you have with others during your day, from casual acquaintances to colleagues and friends to your closest and dearest loved ones.

Your anxiety may be very strong in social situations, perhaps showing up as physical tension or fear of being judged or rejected. Even if you feel lonely, fear of being awkward or not measuring up may lead you to isolate yourself. You may feel that you don't know how to express yourself clearly, or you may have a general sense of uneasiness when you're with others and yet long for deeper connection. Social discomfort can manifest as feeling shy or not clever enough in conversation, but it can also manifest as competition, leading you to force your opinions on others or try to convince them that you're right.

In addition to offering approaches that can help you manage distress and develop a greater sense of ease in social situations, this chapter will also help you better understand your attitudes and opinions about yourself and increase your self-awareness and self-respect. Recognizing and acknowledging your own value and sensitivity is, of course, important in and of itself, and it's also valuable in strengthening your interpersonal skills.

What Is Communication?

Communication means many things to many people. It can be defined as exchanging information, imparting a message, developing rapport, or forging a pathway to accessing other people's experience.

Communication isn't necessarily verbal. For example, body language and facial expression are major nonverbal ways of conveying meaning. Communication also doesn't necessarily involve interactions with other people; you can explore it in the ways you connect with a pet or the ways you're nourished by the natural world.

In eight-week MBSR programs, during the sixth class participants deepen their mindfulness practice by exploring how they communicate with others. Often, participants are asked to reflect briefly on what communication means to them individually. Because such a dynamic aspect of the human experience means different things to each person, participants are told that there's no right answer. Rather, each person offers a unique view of the multifaceted crystal we know as communication. Still, there are some commonalities, and many people's responses touch upon connection, being heard or received, truly listening, speaking clearly, closeness, and clarity.

One especially helpful way of understanding communication is to consider that the word can be boiled down to "commune," meaning "to be one with." When you express yourself, you do so in the hope that others will understand and easily receive your meaning. This can lead to frustration, disappointment, and self-doubt when others seemingly don't comprehend—or worse, reject—what you wanted to express. So how can you actually know whether the other person accurately received what you wished to communicate? One way is to check in, asking others what they heard. When you hear your statement reflected back, you'll have a better idea of the message the other person received, and you can then refine your communication as need be. Of course, this works both ways, so when you're the listener, you can help others by saying: "What I heard you say is..."

TRY THIS!

When engaged in dialogue with others, and particularly if you feel anxious about the interaction, try restating what you just heard them say, paraphrasing and summarizing their words. Notice whether they agree with what you say or refine or clarify it. Also bring attention to times when others make an effort to reflect back to you what you just said. In both situations, tune in to how you feel about the quality of your connection. Also notice how you feel in your body and emotions when you take this approach.

The Role of Perception

As you start taking a closer look at some of the anxiety-related challenges you face in social interactions, you'll once again be exploring the role of perception. It's important to investigate how you attribute meaning to social encounters, both when anticipating them and when they occur. What are the lenses you're looking through? Are you seeing a social interaction as a threat, or are you excited to share ideas and opinions? Do you judge yourself as insufficient or perhaps incapable of expressing what you truly want to say? Remaining alert to the judgments of your mind, that internal "meaning making machine," can provide clarity and help you grow stronger in your relationship with yourself, and in interactions with others.

Being mindfully aware of the lenses of your perception is also crucial to discovering the undercurrents of your self-talk—statements to and about yourself that you may interpret as truths rather than simply thoughts that emerge, stay for a while, and eventually pass. Be on the lookout for self-limiting opinions fueled by anxiety, such as *I'm so nervous. What if I have nothing to say?* When you notice them, substitute alternative self-talk that reflects a different possibility, such as *If I'm curious and ask others about their interests, they're likely to engage, and I may learn something.*

Mindful Exploration: Examining Your Lenses

As you approach an interaction, whether social or work related, bring awareness to how you're anticipating the exchange will unfold. How do you imagine you'll communicate? How do you imagine the other person will receive what you have to say? What do you want from this exchange? After reflecting on this upcoming event for a few moments, take some time to consider and answer the following questions.

What are your thoughts about yourself in this upcoming encounter?

____

____

What are your emotions now as you anticipate it?

____

____

Do you perceive the encounter with worry or with wonder?

____

____

What do you hope will happen?

____

____

____

The Body as a Refuge

Remember, bodily sensations exist only in the here and now, whereas the content of thoughts, especially anxious thoughts, may pull you into the future or past. By intentionally noticing what you're sensing in the body, you can kindly and gently escort your attention from anxious thoughts back into the moment in which you're actually living. As you've learned, the breath offers an excellent anchor in the present moment. When you direct attention to your breath, you come home to your present-moment experience, granting yourself a measure of freedom from anxious thoughts and emotions.

This translates readily into social situations. When you feel discomfort or fear about a social encounter, whether in the past, present, or future, bringing awareness to your body can help you work effectively with your anxiety. As you tune in to your body, bring affectionate attention to whatever sensations you discover. Whether tension or shakiness, blushing or nausea, acknowledge what you feel and, as best you can, allow yourself to be just as you are. As you stay present in the unfolding moment, you'll be more grounded and can attend to your emotions and thoughts with greater ease and equanimity. And as you hold your anxious thoughts and emotions within the container of your body, you may be able to more easily and clearly see that doubts or fearful predictions are just thoughts and emotions are just feeling tones, and that both will pass in due time. By coming home to the body, you can offer yourself strong support in being where and how you are.

Andrea's Story

Andrea had endured a long and challenging relationship with her mother-in-law, Rose, who could almost always find something to criticize. The difficulties of the relationship intensified when Rose, who had become legally blind, moved in with Andrea and her husband, Don. Perhaps because of her impaired vision, Rose would stand very close to Andrea as she expressed her opinions about how Andrea should do routine household tasks and raise her children. Filled with tension, anxiety, and dread, Andrea often edged away from these encounters, but that only made Rose come closer once again.

Andrea started feeling anxious whenever she was at home, and her relationship with Don was growing increasingly tense and conflictual. Fearing for her marriage, Andrea asked a friend for advice, and her friend shared how much peace of mind she'd enjoyed since taking an MBSR class. Andrea decided to give it a try, and as the course progressed, she learned about the fight-or-flight reaction and realized that she perceived Rose as a threat. Over time, as she increasingly tuned in to her internal experiences, Andrea understood that her thoughts and emotions were adding to her feeling of being trapped.

One day she decided to meet the situation in a new way. When Rose stood just inches away from Andrea's face and voiced her complaints, Andrea stood firmly where she was and focused on her bodily sensations. Feeling her feet on the floor and focusing on her breath, she was able to stand firm, not pulling away from Rose as usual. She was amazed but pleased when Rose actually eased up and gave Andrea more room. Perhaps the fact that Andrea didn't retreat made Rose feel more heard, so she didn't need to push her case so hard. Somehow, this interchange set the stage for an evolution in their relationship. With time, Andrea was increasingly able to express her point of view and ask Rose for more support, and she could also open to the compassion she felt for Rose's predicament, living in a situation where she had so little control.

TRY THIS!

When you're in a social interaction, whether a chance encounter or a long-planned event, try firmly rooting yourself into your body. Feel your feet on the ground and your breath as it enters and leaves your body. Sense hot or cold you feel and the touch of clothing on your skin. Fully invite yourself into your physical body in the moment. Then extend the same sort of careful attention to the person you're with. What do you notice? Does your experience of the other person change in any way? Does the quality of the interaction seem to change in any way?

Listening to Yourself and Others

In many MBSR groups, participants are invited to reflect upon their experience of being listened to at times when they wanted to share something with another person. Whether their news was joyful or upsetting, they longed to connect. This activity begins with recalling a time when participants felt unheard and then exploring what they experienced in body, emotions, and thoughts. In this scenario, people often express longing and feelings of frustration and anger. Sometimes they feel despondent, wondering why they bothered and feeling that the other person has never been there for them. Next, they consider a time when they felt listened to. In this scenario, people often feel loved and grateful.

It's important to remember that we've all been on both sides of this experience, and even more important to bear in mind that we each have a great gift to give ourselves and others: choosing to listen and receive. Meditation fosters this ability, as it is a process of deeply listening to your own experience of living in the moment. It's a practice of nonjudgmentally receiving whatever arises in awareness and meeting your experience with greater compassion, moment to moment. As you bring these skills to the awareness that all human beings long for some sort of connection, you'll naturally extend the same nonjudgmental compassion to others who wish to share with you. Our life stories may be distinct, but we all share this very basic wish to be seen, heard, and loved.

Mindful Exploration: The Importance of Being Heard

Take a moment now to reflect on being heard. Call to mind a time when you longed to share some news or experience with someone who wasn't really there for you.

What was your experience physically?

What thoughts did you notice?

What emotions were present?

Now reflect on a time when you wanted to share and felt deeply listened to.

What was your experience physically?

What thoughts did you notice?

What emotions were present?

Considering both of these experiences and everything you explored here, what are you aware of? What do you notice in your body, thoughts, and emotions?

____

____

____

____

Wise Speech

Bringing generosity and attentiveness to listening to others (and yourself) is crucial, but it's only half of the equation in mindful communication. The other key is to take care when choosing your words. Before speaking, especially in heated or anxiety-ridden situations, it's helpful to take a moment to connect with your body and any sensations that are present. You might wish to take a mindful, calming breath. Then mindfully consider what to say, keeping these questions in mind:

- Is it true?
- Is it kind?
- Is it useful?
- Is this the right time and place?

To see how this works, consider Phil and Denise. They'd gotten caught in a pattern where, just as Phil was ready to head out the door for work, Denise would somberly say, "I need to talk with you." Phil immediately became frustrated and felt like he was in a no-win situation. At that moment, he didn't have the time to talk, and Denise would take this as a rejection. If he stopped to talk, he'd probably be late to work and get a warning. Yet if he didn't stop to talk, Denise would probably get angry and he'd have more to deal with later. Still, he usually begged off, saying, "I really don't have time for this right now," before heading out the door. This left Denise with the impression that Phil didn't care about what she had to say, and sometimes she pointedly accused him of this.

One day Phil realized that it wasn't a matter of whether he cared about what Denise had to say; it was a matter of timing. This allowed him to refine his response and say, "I really want to hear what you have to say. I care so much for and about you, and at this moment I just can't give you the full attention that you deserve and that I want to offer. Can we plan a time this evening when we can really talk about it and listen to one another?" Hearing Phil's communication, which was both kind and truthful, Denise could be more open to his situation. And by recognizing that the time and place weren't appropriate and trying to agree upon an alternative that would facilitate communication, Phil was doing something useful to address the situation. Ultimately, this new approach of choosing the best time to connect strengthened their relationship and fostered greater intimacy.

Practicing wise speech can be immensely helpful in many ways, including in decreasing anxiety. As you gain skill and facility in wise speech, you'll become increasingly confident that you're approaching your interactions with others with integrity and compassion, no matter what the outcome of the conversation.

The Longing to Connect

When you were an infant, your life depended on committed attention from others. Depending on how your caretakers responded to your needs for food, soothing, or other care, you developed a tendency to generally trust the world or not. If your early environment wasn't safe, you may have learned to lay low, trying not to be seen by your caretakers in an effort to avoid criticism, extreme demands, judgments, or harsh physical treatment.

No matter what your early experience, as you grew older and capable of taking care of yourself, you probably still felt a longing to be attended to and cared for, and to be seen by others for who you were. You may still feel this need pulsing in your relationships. Understanding this and getting to know your own patterns in regard to this longing is a deeper way of knowing yourself. And as you distinguish between your past and present and escape from the confines of old story lines, this will support you in feeling freer in your exchanges with others. So let's explore these patterns more closely.

Sages throughout history have taught that the source of suffering is a desire for things to be a certain way. Holding these desires tightly is often the source of fear and anxiety, both personal and interpersonal. This tendency can manifest in many ways. It can show up as pushing away what's happening in your life, or as resisting, judging, or hating the way it is. It can also be experienced as clinging to what is, not wanting it to change, transform, or go away. But as we all know, that's just the way life is: constantly in flux.

The Buddha called desires for things to be different hungers, and they are as primal as being extremely hungry or thirsty. When you experience such desires you can fixate urgently on fulfilling the craving, much like the physical need to quench profound hunger or thirst. But these hungers often drive us to seek happiness through the fulfillment of desires on a surface level. So even if we obtain what we long for, ultimately it never completely satisfies. It's like eating cotton candy in an attempt to feel full and nourished. With mindfulness, however, we can identify hungers that lead to suffering—which exist at a deep level in all humans—and work with them in ways that will grant you deeper freedom.

When extended to relationships, the hunger for pleasure, validation, and escaping discomfort can become traps—pitfalls that obstruct the pathway to happiness, dominating and damaging the ways we interact and communicate with others.

More specifically, when these hungers are expressed interpersonally, they take three primary forms:

- The hunger for interpersonal pleasure and the urge to escape loneliness
- The hunger to be seen and the urge to know that you exist
- The hunger to not be seen and the urge to escape intimacy

To be clear, there's nothing inherently wrong with enjoying the company of others, delighting in being recognized and appreciated by others, or enjoying solitude and time alone. The hungers point to something much more demanding and are driven by the urge to escape discomfort. For example, being overwhelmed by a strong hunger for interpersonal pleasure can cause people to not experience and appreciate other people as whole human beings and instead use them in an effort to avoid feeling the pain of loneliness.

Because all of this may sound rather abstract, we'll give you an example of each.

The hunger for interpersonal pleasure and the urge to escape loneliness: Sally couldn't stand being alone, especially on a Saturday night. She typically called friends early in the week to set up activities for the weekend so she could feel more secure about not having to be by herself. She wanted to escape the ache of loneliness and went to extremes to get away from that discomfort.

The hunger to be seen and the urge to know that you exist: John craved recognition. As a child he was the class clown. And as an adult he was the life of every party and a constant overachiever at work. He sought acknowledgment from others to counter his fear that if he wasn't seen and appreciated, he didn't count for anything at all.

The hunger to not be seen and the urge to escape intimacy: Luisa avoided social contact at all costs. She declined almost all invitations and wished she never had to talk to anyone. She isolated herself and avoided intimacy, and sometimes she wished she could be invisible.

With mindfulness, you can more clearly see your own interpersonal patterns, including those related to shyness, insecurity, or anxiety. This puts you in a stronger place to unhook from the urge to escape and instead choose a response in keeping with your values in relationships. It also allows you to work more directly and skillfully with the suffering that arises from resistance to life as it is in the moment. In turn, both of these benefits can go a long way toward decreasing anxiety in social situations in the future.

Formal Practice: Insight Dialogue

Even if you have a strong personal practice of mindfulness, your early conditioning and the basic human hungers discussed above can cause you to lose clarity, balance, and ease when in social situations. The intensity of feelings engendered by these hungers can also lead to anxiety. A wonderful avenue to working directly with this dynamic is intentionally practicing interpersonal mindfulness. In his book *Insight Dialogue: An Interpersonal Path to Freedom* (2007), Gregory Kramer, a teacher of Buddhist meditation and founder of the Metta Foundation, offers just such a meditation practice, conducted while in dialogue with another person. This radical and rewarding approach uses interpersonal contact as the focus of meditation, with the intention of deepening awareness and presence together. As you and a companion practice mindfulness while speaking and listening to another, you tap into the potential to recognize your shared humanity. In dialogue, you can touch the innate wholeness, wisdom, and spaciousness inherent in each of you and ease the usually rigid grip on "I," "me," and "mine."

There are six guidelines for this interpersonal practice. They're all interrelated and foster each other. You can work with all of them together or focus on bringing just one or two of these qualities to any given practice. Choosing to engage with even one of these guidelines can enhance being present and skillful in communication. Of course, time and commitment to the spirit of the practice are essential for growth to occur.

- **Pause.** *Create the gap in which you can move from reactivity to mindful choice.*
- **Relax.** *Allow whatever is present to simply be. Scan your body and release any added tension.*
- **Open.** *Widen your lens and become aware of the space available via your senses and contact with others. Open to the spaciousness that embraces and permeates your experience.*
- **Trust what emerges.** *Attend to the experience of constant change and the potential it offers for creativity and a fresh perspective.*
- **Listen deeply.** *Recognize how meaning is carried through not just words, but also body language, expression, and, most of all, being present to one another. Listen deeply to what the other person expresses, and also what you truly mean to express.*
- **Speak the truth.** *Say what is true for you and what you feel in your body in the moment. Speak with honesty and simplicity, rather than giving in to impulses to be clever, funny, or attractive.*

Ask a friend to take some time to engage in mindful communication with you. Set aside at least thirty minutes when both of you can be free from distractions. It's helpful to set a timer for each part of this practice.

Sit facing one another and choose one or more of the guidelines above— pause, relax, open, trust what emerges, listen deeply, and speak the truth—to focus on. Also choose a topic for your contemplation; for example, you might discuss a shared human experience, such as aging, illness, change, judgments, gratitude, generosity, or, yes, even anxiety. Then conduct your mindful conversation as follows:

1. Establish one person as the first speaker.
2. Set a timer for five minutes. During that time, the first speaker addresses the topic, attending to the interaction and chosen guidelines mindfully. The other person listens deeply and mindfully, without responding.
3. Then the listener reflects what he or she heard and anything he or she noticed about the speaker's verbal content and body language.
4. The speaker shares about how it felt to receive his or her meaning as expressed by the listener, in both words and body language. If an analysis or interpretation was given, the speaker may address the accuracy of the listener's reflection.
5. Change roles and repeat steps 2 through 4.
6. Before ending the mindful dialogue, take some time to dialogue about what both of you experienced.

Mindful Journaling

After your first practice of insight dialogue, take a few moments to write about your experience. How did it feel to fully attend to both speaking and listening? What was your experience of connecting with yourself and with your meditation partner? Were you aware of your body while you were speaking and listening? And what is your experience now, as you write?

____

____

____

____

____

____

Informal Practice: Mindful Communication

When you're feeling anxious, informal mindful communication can be very helpful in grounding yourself and connecting to the stream of life around you. When you listen to yourself more deeply, moment to moment, you're coming home to your own self. And as you grow in your capacity to contact your innate goodness and treat yourself kindly, you can approach others in this way more freely. Then, when you engage with others more mindfully, whether in brief, casual encounters or more meaningful and intimate exchanges, you can cultivate generosity and authenticity. Just as anchoring in the breath and body creates a sense of boundary and containment and increases self-knowledge and self-care, informal mindful communication offers connection in the sphere of ordinary interactions. When engaging with others, take a moment to remember the shared human longing to connect, then receive the other person as whole and complete, just as he or she is in the moment. The experience of connecting and listening without judging is a beautiful gift to give to yourself and others and can shift your focus from the downward spiral of anxiety to a more engaged, wholesome, and integrated view.

Planning Your Formal Practice

In this chapter, you learned one new formal practice: insight dialogue. Hopefully you can find a supportive friend or loved one to engage in this practice with you. Because you'll be working with someone else, you will, of course, need to schedule this practice, hopefully doing it at least a couple of times over the next week. On days when you don't practice insight dialogue, we recommend doing a different formal practice, such as mindful breathing, the body scan, mindful yoga, sitting meditation, narrow-gauge walking meditation, or meditation on anxious emotions. Use the following form to note each time you practice and briefly describe your experience (for a downloadable version, visit http://www.newharbinger.com/29736).

Formal Practice Log

Day and time: ____________________

Your experience: ____________________

____

Day and time: ____________________

Your experience: ____________________

____

Day and time: ____________________

Your experience: ____________________

____

Day and time: ____________________

Your experience: ____________________

____

Day and time: ____________________

Your experience: ____________________

____

Day and time: ____

Your experience: ____

____

Day and time: ____

Your experience: ____

____

Closing the Chapter

In this chapter, we explored communication, how the way in which you perceive yourself and others colors your experience, and how this can play a role in anxiety. Along the way, you continued your journey into mindfulness by attending to communication. By choosing to tune in to how you perceive yourself and your interpersonal interactions, you're breaking free from fixed ideas of who you are and what you can be. You also learned the formal practice of insight dialogue, a method of slowing down conversation and bringing mindfulness to interacting with another person. As you continue to practice the approaches in this chapter and connect with your body and breath, you'll become more comfortable interacting with others and in social situations.

Remember, you are not alone. As human beings, we all share the longing to be received and listened to with care and kindness. In the next chapter, we'll travel deeper into this territory with practices that cultivate reconciliation and loving-kindness. These powerful practices will reveal the depths of your heart even more and grant you greater freedom from anxiety.

Chapter 8

Transforming Anxiety with Reconciliation and Loving-Kindness

In the previous chapter you explored mindful interpersonal communication and how it can ease anxiety. You're increasing your capacity to speak from your heart with the compassionate consideration of wise speech. This chapter will further support your sense of ease in being with others and yourself through meditation practices with a focus on reconciliation and loving-kindness. These beautiful practices open the heart to greater joy, compassion, and wisdom and are truly an antidote to anxiety in both mind and body.

Anxiety often involves feelings of separation and isolation, making it nearly impossible to be at ease and feel safe within your own flesh and being. But just as a single candle can dispel the surrounding darkness, so too can love dispel anxiety. Love is more powerful than fear, and the practices in this chapter will open your heart more deeply to love. Practices that engender reconciliation and loving-kindness are like coming home to the sanctuary of a lush oasis, offering the potential for growing connections to yourself and the world.

Reconciliation

Reconciliation is the path to making peace with yourself and the world. Truly, to live and to die with a heart free of resentment, grudges, and ill will would be a crowning accomplishment in life. By practicing reconciliation meditation, you open the door to this possibility. This is a three-faceted practice. The first aspect is to direct reconciliation toward yourself, making peace with all of the ways in which you've felt deficient or inadequate. These feelings often accompany anxiety, with the sense of *If only I weren't so anxious...* This can make it especially difficult to be at home and at peace with yourself. Reconciliation practice can build a bridge to truly experiencing that you're enough just as you are. The second aspect is reconciliation toward those you've hurt. The third is reconciliation toward those who have hurt you.

To be clear, this is a meditation practice, and all of the work of reconciliation is done within yourself. While the practice may eventually lead to outreach to others to make amends for ways in which you've hurt them, that's a separate choice and not part of this practice. And, of course, although you always have the power to forgive those who have hurt you, you have no control over whether others will seek reconciliation with you. However, you can work within yourself, using this threefold practice, to open a hardened and anxious heart, affording yourself some of the deepest healing and freedom possible.

If you harbor grudges and ill will, it will imprison your heart in a kind of solitary confinement. Conversely, letting go of resentment is like an elixir that releases you from the deep pain of separation and disconnection. If you tend to hold on to grudges or conflict, whether with yourself or others, ask yourself now: Do you think you're any happier because of this? Who really suffers? Of course, those are rhetorical questions. We trust you know that holding on to any type of bitterness is toxic to your health and well-being.

Reconciliation with Yourself

To make peace with yourself is truly a gift. Sadly, most people are way too hard on themselves. Often, people who live with anxiety punish themselves for not being able to change or let go of the anxiety. You may blame yourself for all sorts of things going wrong due to your anxiety. You might even have an ongoing mental tape of incriminating self-talk that ceaselessly comments on your anxiety, judging and endlessly evaluating. Truth be told, if you spoke to your friends the way you sometimes speak to yourself, you probably wouldn't have many friends. Of course, it's unlikely that you'd do that, because people tend to offer more kindness to others than they do to themselves. Like most people, you may be your own worst critic and judge.

Cultivating self-compassion is essential to healing this wound, and also to easing the anxious mind. This is where the first step of reconciliation practice comes in: opening to your own heart and making amends for all of the times you've put yourself down or felt inadequate, flawed, deficient, unworthy, unloving, and unlovable.

Once, when Bob was teaching an MBSR class and conducting a group discussion about how hard people can be on themselves, an elderly woman said, "There has not been one single day in my entire adult life when I haven't called myself an asshole." This opened a floodgate, as another person shared, "I call myself a dummy every day," then another said, "I'm always calling myself a failure." As Bob looked around the room, he saw most of the other participants nodding their heads, acknowledging how self-critical they too were. We've all been wounded in life, and many of us have lost our sense of sovereignty or self-worth. Although upbringing often contributes to this sense of inadequacy, it is possible to break free from old stories, and there's no time like the present! It's time to heal your heart and know that you are unique, special, and worthy.

A wise and skillful way to foster reconciliation with yourself is to look back at your life and reflect upon everything you've done, from your birth right up to this present moment, understanding that all of this has played a role in forming you. All of your joys and sorrows, clarity and confusion, pain and beauty, and feelings of deficiency and even anxiety have played a role in bringing you into this moment, here and now, with your wish for healing.

Reconciliation with Those You've Hurt

The second facet of reconciliation meditation is to offer amends to those you've hurt, even those who are no longer living. All of us have hurt someone, and being human, you're no exception. When anxious, it's easy to lash out from a place of self-protection and fear, sometimes unwittingly turning away from others in our deep desire to protect ourselves. Whether you intentionally or unintentionally caused pain, reconciliation will allow your heart to release the pain of hurting another. It will free you from guilt, shame, and remorse and help you to live with a greater sense of ease.

So that you don't judge yourself too harshly in this phase of the practice, it may be helpful to use your hindsight wisdom to look back and see where you were emotionally when you hurt someone. That perspective can help you understand what fueled your actions. You may discover that you were filled with fear, suffering from old wounds, lacking in awareness, or simply needed to protect yourself. From this vantage point, you may see that you were doing the best you could do at that time.

Reconciliation Toward Those Who Have Hurt You

The final facet of reconciliation meditation is to make amends to those who have hurt you. Making peace with being hurt by another, physically or emotionally, is a difficult endeavor. Yet if you want to ease your anxiety and heal yourself, you need to walk through this doorway and extend reconciliation toward those who have hurt you. It's crucial to let go of grudges, resentment, and ill will, as living with a hardened heart is a heavy load to carry. Often, this burden is laced with anxiety about old wrongs, adding to the wall built against others. It's not unusual for people to mentally review situations where they feel they've been wronged. Yet this rehashing can create more anxiety as we encounter the sense of being wronged, even if only in the mind. This essentially shuts our hearts away, keeping ourselves and those we love from knowing and feeling what we have to offer. Plus, the more bitterness you put out into the world, the more you'll agonize. Even though you're pointing one finger at the person you blame for hurting you, there are three other fingers pointing back at you. When you harbor resentment, you're actually the one who's tangled in suffering. The other person may not know or may not care. The good news is, you're also the one with the power to untangle yourself, which will help you shed your anxiety.

Lightening your load of resentment against others is immensely freeing—and sometimes also immensely difficult. Again, you can benefit from hindsight wisdom. Just as you reflected on the forces that may have played a role in the instances when you hurt others, consider what factors may have been involved when others have hurt you. Perhaps their actions were born of unawareness, fear, or insecurity. In this way, you can foster willingness to extend reconciliation toward those who have hurt you.

MINDFUL PAUSE

Pause for a moment to invite reconciliation into your heart. Breathe mindfully and feel into how, with each exhalation, you can release resentment, and how, with each inhalation, you can bring in more ease of being. As the burden of grudges and criticism, including self-criticism, falls away, feel the freedom of being more at peace with yourself and others. May all beings dwell with peace.

Formal Practice: Reconciliation Meditation

Now we'll introduce you to the formal practice of reconciliation meditation. To allow you to fully experience this meditation without referring to the book, we recommend that you listen to the downloadable audio version, which is available at http://www.newharbinger.com/29736 (see the back of this book for instructions on how to access it). However, you can also simply read the text below. If you do this, read through the entire script first to familiarize yourself with the practice, then do the practice, referring back to the text as needed and pausing briefly after each paragraph. Take about twenty minutes for the practice. You can do it in a seated position, standing, or even lying down. Choose a position in which you can be comfortable and alert.

Take a few moments to pause and check in with yourself, acknowledging whatever you're feeling physically, mentally, and emotionally... This may be the first time today that you're stopping to check in with yourself to get a sense of how you're doing. As you feel into your body and mind, just allow whatever is there and let it be. There's no need to fix or solve anything. Just acknowledge whatever is in your direct experience.

Now gradually become mindful of your breath...breathing in and knowing that you're breathing in...breathing out and knowing that you're breathing out. Just take your life one inhalation and one exhalation at a time. Being present.

Now gently shift from your breath to feeling into your heart and reflecting on the preciousness and fragility of life... As you sense into your heart, try to hold it with great care and tenderness, opening to yourself with self-compassion. Let this be a time to make peace with yourself and end the war of self-loathing. Feel how, just like all beings, you are imperfectly perfect, just as you are.

Open to the hindsight wisdom that can understand how all of your past, with all of its joys and sorrows, has led you into this moment. It has all been a part of what brought you here, now. Open to deep reconciliation with your past, knowing that your woundedness and lack of awareness contributed to your sense of unworthiness, inadequacy, whatever closed your heart to yourself. Let this be a time to open your heart to deep self-compassion and love for yourself. Gently say to yourself, "May I be at ease and at peace. May I open to deep compassion for myself just as I am." Rest in this reconciliation with yourself for a few minutes.

Now begin to expand this sense of reconciliation, extending it out to those you've hurt, whether through words, actions, or thoughts. Open your heart and, within yourself, make amends to those you've wounded in some way. Use your hindsight wisdom to reflect on how your actions were fueled by fear, anxiety, lack of awareness, or the need to protect yourself. Feel your heart becoming lighter and more at ease with the pain you've caused others as you understand where you were then and the pain you were experiencing within your own heart…extending reconciliation to those you've hurt… Rest in this sense of reconciliation with those you've hurt for a few minutes.

Now begin to open to reconciliation toward those who have hurt you. This may feel very difficult at first. Know that this practice will help release your heart from anxiety and foster deep healing and peace. It's a pathway to increasing your own well-being and ease as you free yourself from the burden of living with resentment, grudges, and ill will. So feel into your heart and open to reconciliation toward those who have hurt you. Reflect on how, just as your own fear and lack of awareness allowed you to hurt others, this may also be true for those who have hurt you. The source of their hurtful actions is their own pain and woundedness. Rest in this sense of reconciliation with those who have hurt you for a few minutes… May we all find the gateways into our hearts and experience reconciliation.

As you're ready to end this meditation, congratulate yourself for taking this time to open your heart to reconciliation with yourself, with those you've hurt, and with those who have hurt you. May all beings dwell within this peace.

Mindful Journaling

Right after your first practice of reconciliation meditation, take a few moments to write about your experience. How did it go for you? What did you notice in your body, mind, and emotions? Did you experience any challenges? If so, how did you work with them? Did the practice touch or open your heart? And how are you feeling right now?

Sue's Story

As Sue was growing up, her mother criticized her often, which made her feel anxious and inadequate. It seemed she could hardly do anything right. Given this oppressive and negative environment, Sue could hardly wait to leave home. As soon as she graduated from high school, she married Joe, her high school sweetheart. The early years of their marriage were happy, and before long, they had five wonderful children. Sue was a devoted wife and mother.

Then, after twenty years of marriage, Sue found out that Joe had been cheating on her, and he eventually left to be with another woman. Of course, this would be painful for anyone, but Sue's difficulties were heightened because she blamed herself for the situation. She felt she had brought a lot of anxiety into her marriage, and that not feeling sure of herself had played a role in Joe's loss of affection. For example, her anxiety manifested in difficulties with decision making, even about things as seemingly minor as what color to paint the bedroom. She tended to anxiously ruminate about such decisions for days on end. Her anxiety manifested in other ways as well, and all in all, it created a tense environment to live in. Then, when her marriage was falling apart, Sue became consumed by even more anxiety. She thought that, just as her mother had told her so many times, she couldn't do anything right, so it must be her fault.

Yet, even though she blamed herself for her anxiety, she tried to hurt Joe to make him pay for leaving her. She told her kids that he was awful and tried to turn them against him. Secretly, Sue felt like her life was over and considered suicide, but she knew she could never do it because her kids needed her. Broken and dejected, she finally sought help from a therapist.

Sue's therapist introduced her to mindfulness meditation, and she found it helpful for beginning to ease her painful emotions. Still, she continued to struggle with anxiety, low self-esteem, and resentment. When she described these feelings to her therapist, he suggested that reconciliation meditation might be helpful and explained the threefold practice.

When Sue did the first part of the practice, she noticed familiar feelings of anxiety and self-loathing and the belief that she couldn't do anything right. She realized that this belief had become so strong that she never even questioned that there could be another way of viewing herself. Sue also began to understand how this story had played out with Joe, as she repeatedly told herself that any problems were her fault because she wasn't competent, smart, pretty, and on and on—self-talk that only increased her anxiety and detracted from the quality of her relationships, especially with Joe. As Sue opened her heart to greater self-compassion, she realized that she had many strengths, including all of the abilities that had allowed her to raise five great kids, and to keep doing that even when Joe left her. She turned toward the wounded part within her with great tenderness and kindness and began to heal her self-loathing. This helped her feel more safe and secure and less anxious as she discovered the beauty and strength within her.

When Sue engaged in the second facet of reconciliation meditation, making amends to those she'd hurt, she realized she needed to address all the pain she'd caused Joe due to her feelings of angst and betrayal. This was very difficult at first, because she felt he deserved to be punished, but she also understood that her vindictiveness was hurting not just Joe, but also her kids and even herself. She recognized that despite Joe's betrayal, it was important to her not to cause others to suffer. Again, she opened to her own heart, this time making amends to herself for causing pain to another.

Then Sue turned to the third facet of reconciliation meditation: reconciliation with those who had hurt her. She reflected on how holding grudges created pain within her and realized that neutralizing her resentment toward both Joe and her mother was the pathway to easing that pain and letting go of her guardedness and anxiety. As Sue sat with this reflection, she saw that, although she hadn't realized it, her upbringing and lack of awareness played a big role in her reactivity and desire to hurt Joe, and she recognized that something similar was probably true for Joe. She knew that Joe had always been plagued by insecurity and wondered if that had driven him to seek out other women—to prove his manhood. She also saw that as long as Joe looked outside of himself for validation, he would never truly find it. With this understanding, Sue felt a wave of compassion for Joe and could truly extend forgiveness to him with the wish that he might someday find his own heart.

From that day forward, Sue felt a kind of peace she'd never known. She never again had a bad word to say about Joe and always wished him the best. She went on to live a long life and was the grand matriarch of her family, delighting in her fifteen grandchildren. And when she died, Sue left this world with no resentment and with peace in her heart. Hers was a life well lived.

Loving-Kindness Meditation

Clearing the heart with reconciliation sets the stage for beginning to practice loving-kindness meditation. In Pali, the language of early Buddhism, the word for loving-kindness is *metta*—a word that also means "friendliness," "goodwill," "benevolence," or "that which softens the heart." It's similar to the spirit of the Hawaiian word "aloha," which carries a sense of loving everyone, even those who don't speak kindly to you. "Aloha" means not giving up on others, recognizing that they may be having a bad day, and trying again the next day.

The Origins of Loving-Kindness Meditation

The story of how the practice of loving-kindness came to be is a wonderful tale that nicely conveys the feeling of this beautiful practice. During the Buddha's time, a small group of monks journeyed to a remote forest to practice meditation. For the first few days everything went well. The forest was quiet and protected from the hot sun, and a stream for drinking and bathing ran peacefully through it.

Unbeknownst to the monks, the forest was inhabited by tree spirits, and once they realized the monks weren't leaving anytime soon, they became annoyed. In an effort to frighten the monks away, the tree spirits, which usually dwelled in beautiful, radiant bodies, transformed themselves into frightening forms, emitted a stinking stench, and screeched and howled in a terrifying way. In short order, the monks came to the conclusion that the forest was haunted and fled, believing they couldn't practice meditation there.

Upon their return to their monastery, the Buddha asked them why they'd come back. When the monks explained what had happened, the Buddha suggested that they return to the forest and practice a new form of meditation, then instructed them in *metta*, or loving-kindness meditation. He told them to practice the meditation every step of the way as they journeyed back to the forest, which they did.

When the tree spirits saw the monks returning to their forest, they were outraged and immediately resumed their frightening forms, emitted an even worse stench, howled and screeched more loudly, and prepared to attack. Nevertheless, the monks continued to advance, practicing loving-kindness with each step toward the forest, wishing the tree spirits and all beings well. As the tree spirits waited, they began to feel a sense of peace, like a gentle, benevolent breeze that brought calmness and ease. They sat in their trees feeling serene and happy, and without even discussing it, they all transformed back into their radiant, beautiful forms. Then some gathered water, others cleared the forest paths, and still others made a fire to greet the monks.

When they met the monks, they were so profoundly moved by the effects of loving-kindness that they invited the monks to dwell with them in the forest. They asked the monks to teach them the practice of *metta*, and soon they were all practicing together, experiencing ever-greater depths of peace and freedom.

Qualities of Loving-Kindness

The story of the origins of loving-kindness speaks to its universal qualities as a boundless kind of love that knows no bias. It can be compared to the sun, moon, or stars in that it shines its light on all beings without exception. The loving-kindness practice is a wonderful antidote for anxiety. Fear, anxiety, worry, and panic cannot endure when your heart is filled with love. It's said that when you practice loving-kindness, you'll sleep peacefully, enjoying sweet dreams, and awaken with a sense of calm. It's also said that this practice will cause you to be loved by many and protected from both inner and outer harm, and that you'll be joyful and bright in life and die with peace in your heart.

Traditionally, the practice of loving-kindness follows a particular sequence in which you first cultivate loving-kindness toward yourself, then gradually expand outward to benefactors (teachers), near and dear ones (family, friends, and community), neutral ones (acquaintances and strangers), difficult ones (sometimes termed "enemies"), those who are suffering, all living beings in this world, and finally throughout the universe, to all beings everywhere. Initially, it may feel difficult to extend loving-kindness to difficult ones—the people you find challenging. Know that ongoing practice of both loving-kindness meditation and the preceding reconciliation meditation will increase your capacity to do so.

Traditional phrases for extending loving-kindness at all of these levels include "May you be happy," "May you be safe from harm," "May you be healthy," and "May you be at peace." However, the key is to use phrases that resonate with you so that you can fully immerse yourself in the spirit and intention of the meditation, so feel free to come up with your own phrases if you like.

What If You Don't Feel Loving?

While practicing loving-kindness meditation, there may be times when you don't feel loving at all, or perhaps feel the opposite. Rest assured that it's normal to have feelings like resentment, sadness, envy, anger, fear, or confusion during this practice. When Bob began practicing loving-kindness meditation, he had a nickname for it, "hating-kindness meditation," because it brought up all of his old pain and resentment. As time went on, he began to recognize and understand that whatever stood in the way of feeling loving-kindness was his teacher, clearly revealing where he was stuck, and also showing him that he needed to bring more attention to healing his wounded and hardened heart.

If you ever feel stuck in anger or resentment while practicing loving-kindness meditation, the first step is to acknowledge your feelings and allow yourself to feel them. The very fact that you're aware of these feelings and have begun to work with them sets you on the path to freedom. It's an entirely different approach than reacting to difficult feelings and creating even more pain and separation. Once you become aware that you're entangled in hard feelings, you can begin to free yourself from them. With awareness, you begin to break the cycle of reactivity and open the door to understanding and loving-kindness.

MINDFUL PAUSE

Pause for a moment to invite loving-kindness into your heart. Breathe mindfully, and with each inhalation, fill your being with loving-kindness for yourself as you are in this moment. With each exhalation, feel yourself releasing hard-heartedness, becoming lighter and more peaceful with each breath.

Formal Practice: Loving-Kindness Meditation

When you first begin practicing loving-kindness meditation, it's important to practice in a place that feels safe and comfortable for you. It could be in your bedroom or backyard, in a beautiful spot in nature, or even at work—wherever you feel safe. Sometimes it's helpful to begin by reflecting on a time in your life when you felt safe and at ease so you can bring those feelings into your heart as you practice loving-kindness meditation.

To allow you to fully experience this meditation without referring to the book, we recommend that you listen to the downloadable audio instructions, which are available in three versions—fifteen, thirty, and forty-five minutes—at http://www.newharbinger.com/29736. However, you can also simply read the text below. If so, read through the entire script first to familiarize yourself with the practice, then do the practice, referring back to the text as needed and pausing briefly after each paragraph. You can do this meditation in a seated position, standing, or even lying down. Choose a position in which you can be comfortable and alert.

As you practice this meditation, feel free to make up your own phrases if those in the instructions don't resonate with you. It's important that you truly invest yourself in the practice of loving-kindness meditation, rather than just reciting set words or phrases in a formulaic way.

Take a few moments right now to pause and check in with yourself, acknowledging whatever you're feeling physically, mentally, and emotionally. This might be the first time today that you're stopping to check in with yourself, so just allow whatever is within you and let it be. There's no need to judge or analyze whatever is present.

Now gently direct your attention to your breathing. As you breathe in, be aware of breathing in, and as you breathe out, be aware of breathing out...breathing normally and naturally and being mindful of your breath wherever you feel it most prominently and distinctly in your body... Breathing in and breathing out, one breath at a time.

Now gently bring your awareness into your heart and feel whatever is there, physically or emotionally, and just let it be. The heart is a great reminder of how precious and fragile life is, offering an entryway into deeper compassion and love for yourself and for all beings... Open into your own heart and life with compassion, kindness, and love. Take some time to feel into the beautiful qualities of loving-kindness, a boundless love that, like the sun, moon, and stars, shines on all living beings without distinction or prejudice.

Now open to receive this love into your heart, directing it toward yourself and letting it nourish every aspect of your being. As you open into your heart, repeat the following phrases, or whatever loving-kindness phrases you choose, and try to experience them within yourself.

May I be safe.
May I be healthy.
May I have ease of body and mind.
May I be at peace.

Now expand the field of loving-kindness to include your teachers, mentors, benefactors, and others who have inspired you, again repeating these phrases or whatever phrases work for you.

May my teachers, mentors, and benefactors be safe.
May my teachers, mentors, and benefactors be healthy.
May my teachers, mentors, and benefactors have ease of body and mind.
May my teachers, mentors, and benefactors be at peace.

Now once again expand the field of loving-kindness to include those who are near and dear to you, such as your family, friends, and community.

May my near and dear ones be safe.
May my near and dear ones be healthy.
May my near and dear ones have ease of body and mind.
May my near and dear ones be at peace.

Now further extend the field of loving-kindness to people you feel neutral toward, such as acquaintances and strangers.

May my neutral ones be safe.

May my neutral ones be healthy.
May my neutral ones have ease of body and mind.
May my neutral ones be at peace.

Now consider extending loving-kindness to those whom you find difficult or challenging. Initially, it may feel almost impossible to send loving-kindness to this group. If you feel this way, consider whether you benefit from holding resentments. Does holding grudges support your health and well-being? Given how toxic resentment can be, consider opening your heart and extending loving-kindness even to your difficult ones. Extend the wish that they may find the pathway into their own hearts, growing in awareness and love. Then, as best you can, gently send loving-kindness to your difficult ones.

May my difficult ones be safe.
May my difficult ones be healthy.
May my difficult ones have ease of body and mind.
May my difficult ones be at peace.

Now send loving-kindness to everyone who is suffering, anxious, or going through challenging times in life—those you know personally and those you don't. Let your loving-kindness and wishes for healing extend to everyone who's in pain.

May all who are suffering be safe.
May all who are suffering be healthy.
May all who are suffering have ease of body and mind.
May all who are suffering be at peace.

Continuing to open your heart to its bountiful capacity of loving-kindness, now extend your wishes for well-being to all human beings and beyond, to all living beings, whether near or far, and even to those who are yet to be born. Extend loving-kindness to all creatures great and small, spreading your wishes for well being in all directions.

May all beings in this world be safe.
May they all be healthy.
May all beings in this world have ease of body and mind.
May they all be at peace.

Finally, extend this boundless love even further, throughout the solar system and the entire universe, sending out wishes that all beings everywhere be safe and healthy and dwell in peace.

May all beings throughout the universe be safe.
May they all be healthy.
May all beings throughout the universe have ease of body and mind.
May they all be at peace.

Now gently return your focus to your breath, feeling your whole body as you breathe in and out. Feel how the body rises and expands with each inhalation and releases with each exhalation. Feel your body as a unified being, connected, whole, and free of anxiety…being at ease and at peace as you breathe in and out.

As you're ready to end this meditation, congratulate yourself for taking the time to open your heart to yourself and all living beings. Then gently wiggle your toes and fingers, open your eyes, and slowly reconnect with the outer environment around you.

Mindful Journaling

Right after your first practice of loving-kindness meditation, take a few moments to write about your experience. How did it go for you? What did you notice in your body, mind, and emotions? Did you experience any challenges? If so, how did you work with them? What were you touched by as you practiced? And how are you feeling right now?

____

____

____

____

____

____

Planning Your Practice

In this chapter you learned two new formal practices: reconciliation meditation and loving-kindness meditation. Please practice them daily for the next week, perhaps alternating which one you practice from day to day. You are also welcome to continue practicing any of the formal mindfulness meditations introduced earlier, to further build your practice. As usual, we recommend scheduling your practice times in advance and making a commitment to keep these appointments with yourself. Then, use the following form to note each time you practice and briefly describe your experience. (Find a downloadable version of it at http://www.newharbinger.com/29736).

Mindful Reconciliation Meditation and Loving-Kindness Meditation Practice Log

Day and time: ____

Your experience: ____

____

Day and time: ____

Your experience: ____

____

Day and time: ____

Your experience: ____

____

Day and time: ____

Your experience: ____

____

Day and time: ____

Your experience: ____

____

Day and time: ____

Your experience: ____

____

Closing the Chapter

We believe that learning and practicing reconciliation meditation and loving-kindness meditation can be very helpful in diminishing anxiety. Learning to make peace with yourself, with those you've hurt, and with those who have hurt you can be profoundly healing. It's impossible to overestimate the powers of reconciliation and love. These practices can soften even the hardest and most fearful of hearts. Both foster a benevolent and beautiful acceptance of yourself, your experience, and others.

In the next chapter, you'll learn some MBSR strategies for bringing more mindfulness to day-to-day living, including making mindful lifestyle choices and being sensitive to what's called for in the moment. But first, take a moment to reflect on this beautiful poem by Miller Williams (1997, 55; reprinted with permission). It offers compelling insight into why we would all do well to extend reconciliation and compassion even to those we find most difficult or challenging.

Have Compassion

Have compassion for everyone you meet
even if they don't want it. What seems conceit,
bad manners, or cynicism is always a sign
of things no ears have heard, no eyes have seen.
You do not know what wars are going on
down there where the spirit meets the bone.

Chapter 9

MBSR Tools for Day-to-Day Living

If you've been following this book closely and doing your best to incorporate both the formal and informal practices into your daily routine, it is likely that you've been experiencing improvements in your anxiety—and probably in other areas in your life as well. This may be showing up in dramatic ways or more subtly. As you become more centered and at ease, with less anxiety and more choice in how to respond to challenges, this new state can feel so natural that you almost forget that, in similar situations in the past, you might have been more anxious and reactive. And if you've occasionally missed a day or two of practice, you might also have noticed how that impacted you. In fact, sometimes it's only when people miss a few days of practice that they realize they are indeed experiencing benefits.

This chapter offers some perspectives on how to weave the principles and practices of mindfulness into your daily life to support your growing sense of wholesome presence, allowing the seeds you've planted to firmly take root and flourish. In particular, we'll look at how your choices can better support your deepest intentions.

The Ongoing Evolution of Your Mindfulness Practice

There's no end to this exploration. Once you begin practicing mindfulness in earnest and feel a commitment to it as a way of life, your practice and your intentions in practicing may shift. Rather than seeing mindfulness primarily as a way to relieve anxiety, you may discover that you want to develop or explore different parts of yourself—parts that have perhaps been languishing in darkness or been put on hold due to the demands of anxiety. Your life can be an ongoing adventure as you work within yourself and develop your skills in mindfulness, allowing everything inside you to fully bloom.

In eight-week MBSR programs, around weeks six and seven participants feel both a growing sense of independence and also some worry about what will happen when they don't have the class to support their practice. Using this book is different, since its guidance is always available, but as you enter the final chapters, you may quite naturally wonder about what's next. In addition, you may discover you tend to react to endings (even the ending of a self-paced program in a book) in ways that can spark anxiety. As with all awareness, this can shed light on your experience and help guide your process.

Mindful Exploration: Continuing to Grow Your Mindfulness Practice

Below are some questions that you may be asking yourself as you near the end of the book or that may spark your interest in an ongoing exploration of mindfulness. Taking the time to write about your thoughts regarding these questions, or others you may have, can help you grow and refine your practice. You might also wish to take some time to consider where you are right now compared to when you began, perhaps even rereading some of what you've written in your work with this book. This will help you choose your path forward.

How will you proceed without the guidance of the book?

____

____

____

What's really working for you?

____

____

____

How can you expand your learning? What else can you do to deepen your self-knowledge?

____

____

____

Gloria's Story

Gloria felt that she had been anxious her entire life, though she'd never received a formal diagnosis. She always felt like she was scrambling to catch up, seldom in tune with herself or her life or at ease within herself. She tended to breathe shallowly, and her eyes often darted about, as if seeking a safe place to land. She had engaged in therapy and it had been helpful in increasing her understanding of many of her patterns, but she struggled when it came to changing those patterns.

She decided to take an MBSR class, and given her long-term problems with anxiety, she was more than willing to commit the time required. She brought great discipline and focus to her practice, but as the end of the course loomed, Gloria had a major realization, which she shared in class: "I totally made the course the top priority in my life, going to bed early so I could get up and practice before starting my day, weeding out old activities to make time for informal practice during my day, using mindful communication, and bringing more care, love, and compassion to myself. I've really benefited from all of this, and I'm feeling so much calmer and more content. But now that the course is winding down, I see that I've been doing this for the course, and I realize that I have to do it for my life."

With a pained look on her face, she continued, "I love movies. I love novels and reading. I love nightlife and going into the city for excitement. I love intellectual discussions and intense conversations. But through these eight weeks, I've seen that some of those activities don't really support me, at least not as I've been approaching them. It's been fine to put them aside for eight weeks, but I don't want to never go into the city for excitement or never have late-night conversations with friends." She was in a real quandary about this, but as she continued to talk about it, she realized that she needed to explore these activities and their impacts in a mindful way. As she considered this, she grew calmer: "I know I could be more discriminating in what I read and in getting to bed at a more reasonable time most nights. Truthfully, some of the people I've had intense conversations with aren't people I feel genuinely close to. And since starting this program, I've been surprised by some of the deep conversations I've had about my practice and awareness with the people in my life I do care about."

Over the next week, Gloria explored her activities and inclinations. When she returned to class the following week, she acknowledged a feeling of sadness about letting go of some of the activities she'd once craved. Then she acknowledged how her mindfulness practice had helped her get in touch with a sense of more fullness and wholeness inside of herself, separate from her activities, and this brought her an entirely new perspective on what was most nourishing for her whole being.

Nourishing Yourself at All Levels

Gloria's story is a good example of how making a change in one area of your life can have a ripple effect in other areas. As your mindfulness practice brings you a new sense of confidence and centeredness, you may realize that some of your activities and approaches to life don't truly support you. Yet you may have come to rely on these activities or choices for entertainment or to fill gaps in your life, and, like Gloria, you may have a sense of grief about letting them go. As you examine these aspects of your life and consider making changes, be gentle with yourself and express appreciation for your increased capacity to meet yourself and make space to discover what is truly nourishing for you. Also recognize that it takes time to shift old habits and priorities, and forgive yourself when you don't change as quickly as you think you should.

Of course, we're all different, and what nourishes one person may be entirely unhelpful for another. In addition, there are many different ways in which we nourish ourselves, from the purely physical to the social to the intellectual. The next exercise will help you explore this to discover what truly nourishes you.

Mindful Exploration: Wise Nourishment for All Levels of Your Being

In this exercise, we invite you to check in with yourself regarding the ways in which you nourish yourself. What are you taking in? What is the impact of a particular food, activity, or person? Really take your time as you reflect on whether you're satisfied with how you're being nourished in each area. Are there changes you might make to improve your overall well-being, health, and sense of ease? In each area, you might bring particular focus to how your choices affect your anxiety. As you engage in this exploration, please bear in mind that the focus isn't on fixing something that's broken; rather, you're taking an honest look at how you'd like to shape your life as you move forward, building on the skills and resources you're cultivating with mindfulness. This might stimulate a great deal of thought, so feel free to reflect and write for a while, then take a break. As you're ready, you can return to continue this exploration.

Food and drink. Are you satisfied with the quality and quantity of what you're eating and drinking? Do you respond to your levels of hunger and thirst appropriately? Are there times when you overeat or undereat? Are there times when you're uncomfortable with your food or beverage choices? What about alcohol, caffeine, or other substances that might play a role in your anxiety or your well-being in general? What are some small, gentle steps you might take in an effort to better meet your genuine needs in the area of food and drink?

____

____

____

Exercise and movement. How much time each week do you set aside to move your body? Are you satisfied with this amount of time? Do you tend exercise excessively or insufficiently? Are there ways you could be more sensitive to your body's needs for movement? Are there physical activities you'd like to try that you've been avoiding out of fear? How might you encourage yourself to try them? Are there activities that might help you burn off nervous energy?

____

____

____

Sleep. How much sleep do you get each night, on average? Do you tend to sleep too much or not enough? Do you wake up feeling refreshed? Are you responsive to your body's need for rest, making sure to get to bed early enough that you can get sufficient sleep? Might changes to your sleep habits help ease your anxiety? Are you willing to bring kindness to this area of your life as you work to get enough rest amidst your other commitments and demands?

____

____

____

Media. Here, we address more classic forms of media as sources of information, news, culture, and entertainment, such as newspapers, magazines, television, movies, and books. (In the next question, you'll consider the vast and rapidly expanding world of electronic and Internet-based information.) On average, how much time do you spend taking in media on a daily basis? What value do you get from the media? How do you feel about the quality of your choices? Are you using media to fill time and ease boredom? Do you turn to media to distract you when you feel agitated? Do you turn to media to avoid other activities? Are there steps you'd like to take to change your relationship with media?

____

____

____

Technology. Here, we address e-mail, social media such as Facebook and Twitter, and computers, smartphones, and other electronic devices. How do you relate to and use technology? How much time do you spend on the computer or a smartphone? Do you feel pressure to engage in social media? Do you feel like you're missing something if you don't check in frequently? How do you feel while using these forms of technology, and how do you feel afterward?

____

____

____

Relationships. Which relationships deepen your connection to yourself or enliven you with a sense of joy, connection, or fresh perspective? Are there any relationships that tend to bring more negativity or conflict into your life? Of course, all long-lived close relationships are punctuated by times of distance, conflict, or stress, so examine these relationships in their larger context. While it can be highly worthwhile to make changes in how you nourish yourself socially, be aware that when making changes in long-term relationships, it's important to be thoughtful and compassionate, including in regard to relationships that are difficult or even toxic.

____

____

____

Time. More generally speaking, how do you spend your time? Are you making choices that support your deepest intentions and priorities and increase your sense of calm and well-being? If not, what's standing in the way? And if you are making positive choices, do you actively acknowledge the ways in which you're living to the fullest, taking opportunities to celebrate and consciously enjoy your choices? You might also consider the balance between work and recreational activities, time alone and time with others, and time spent engaging in enjoyable hobbies and service-related activities, such as volunteering, contributing to your community, and so on.

____

____

____

Phil's Story

After practicing mindful yoga and the body scan for several weeks, Phil found that his stress level and reactivity were much lower, even though he still had lingering feelings of anxiety. Within himself, he felt more space for his anxious feelings to simply be, without distracting him from the fuller experience of his life. Phil's wife, Maria, had been attending a yoga class, and after giving it some thought, Phil decided to go with her and try some classes. He was nervous, because being around strangers was one of the things he found most difficult and anxiety provoking, but from the first class, he was pleasantly surprised. He'd always avoided group sports and fitness activities because he felt physically awkward, but he discovered that he could do some of the poses quite well, and actually more proficiently than others could. This challenged some of his habitual thoughts about himself and his body and gave him a boost in confidence.

In addition, during yoga classes Phil felt quite calm, which was totally unlike his typical experience in being around strangers and in social contexts. Along with helping him better connect with his body, this calmness also allowed him to enjoy being with others. And because of the context of the class, he didn't feel the typical pressure to relate in a social way. After a few weeks, he started feeling comfortable enough to initiate conversations with other participants. As a bonus, the class also offered Phil a different avenue for sharing experiences with Maria. This enhanced the sense of intimacy and connection in their marriage—something Phil hadn't expected but that he cherished.

Informal Practice: Bringing Mindfulness to Daily Activities

In earlier chapters, you learned a variety of informal practices that can support you in working with anxiety more skillfully while also connecting more deeply with your moment-to-moment experience and living more authentically. In addition, you can explore bringing greater mindfulness to day-to-day activities to increase your capacity to attend to and focus on your experience.

To begin, choose an activity you do every day. Keep it simple: brushing your teeth, walking the dog, making your morning beverage, showering, cooking, or something similarly straightforward. Then, when you do this activity, bring your full attention to the experience: see, hear, smell, taste, and feel whatever is there to be sensed. Taste the toothpaste, see your dog's fur gleaming in the sun, feel warm water from the shower, smell the coffee, hear the onions sizzling as you sauté them. Use your senses to immerse yourself fully in the activity.

As you repeat this activity day after day, continue to bring beginner's mind to it. Rather than seeing it as just another thing you must do, notice how it feels to be more fully alive to this ordinary activity. After working with one activity for several weeks, consider expanding and including another, gradually increasing the reach of mindfulness in your daily life.

One woman in an MBSR class reported that mindfully feeding her dog in the morning progressively changed her whole morning routine as she slowed down and experienced herself and the early hours of her day. After several days of mindfully feeding her dog, her sense of care and presence expanded, and she began to attend to herself and her environment in the same way. Spontaneously, she found it easier to clean up after breakfast, rather than leaving the dirty dishes in the sink for later. Leaving her kitchen in a state of cleanliness eased her out the door with more calmness. And when she got home in the evening, she found the tidy environment welcoming, offering an invitation to cook and relax after work—a time that had often been rushed and anxious in the past. All of this from just feeding her dog mindfully!

Another woman opted to wash her face mindfully each night. In class, she shared that instead of looking at herself with a critical eye, noting the signs of aging and her "imperfections," she began to see herself in a new light, appreciating her age and what she'd been through and accomplished. As her hands were sudsing up her face and she looked into her eyes in the mirror, she offered herself kindness and love.

Bringing Curiosity to What's Called for in the Moment

As mindfulness becomes a way of life through your formal and informal practices, you'll increasingly tune in to an ongoing awareness of what's called for in the moment. By being present to yourself in this way, you continue to broaden your mindfulness skills and greet your experiences with a sense of curiosity and self-compassion.

This kind of moment-to-moment awareness was immensely helpful to Terri, who was going through a rough time after a long-term relationship ended. She was experiencing a lot of anxiety whenever she was away from home for more than two or three hours. At those times, her urges to go home weren't just inconvenient; they also were distressing because they made her doubt her ability to conduct herself as an adult in the world.

One evening when Terri was standing in line at the grocery store, feeling anxious to get home and impatient at how slowly the line was moving, she decided to do a brief body scan. As she got in touch with the knot in her stomach and the tightness in her brow and jaw, she instinctively shifted her weight to come into mountain pose. Rather than standing with one hip jutting out and the hand basket resting on her leg, she realigned her hips and brought her weight evenly into balance on both feet. She moved the basket in front of her, equally supported by both hands. Her breath deepened as she did this, and the tightness in her brow and jaw softened just a bit.

In that moment, Terri looked up and, for the first time since she'd come into the grocery store, saw the other people around her: a mother with two fussy kids; a middle-aged man coming home from a long day of construction or trade work, his fingers grimy with grease and his face reflecting a day of toil. She also took in the clerk, hurriedly swiping the items across the scanner and barely looking up from the task.

Although Terri didn't know any of these people personally, she suddenly saw them with a realness and depth she could relate to. She recognized that they too were feeling the stress of a long day and longed to be at home, comfortable and with some measure of ease. As she realized this, she felt more connected, content, and at home right where she was. She realized that she had entered into her own presence, and that this was the real sense of home she'd been missing. With her posture strong and her vision clear, she silently extended loving-kindness to those around her and to herself.

When your formal practice has taken root, as it had with Terri, the possibility of waking up, being present, and remembering to check in with your body, your breath, and your own intimate experience is increasingly likely. And if this happens when you're out in the world, it can shift your perception. The shift may not always be profound or dramatic, but it always contributes to a greater sense of wholeness and presence. Whether you're talking with neighbors, trying to get your kids out the door on a rainy morning when everyone has overslept, or sitting with someone who's sick or dying, mindfulness can be a steady companion, offering quiet but powerful connection to you and those you're with.

In the end, all mindfulness practices—formal and informal—come down to a way of being in the world. It's a way of being that reflects a sense of flexibility, innate wholeness, and connection to life. In a very real sense, the entire endeavor can be captured in one seemingly simple question: What's called for now? In this way, you can make informed choices about what's nourishing for you moment to moment—choices about what's on your plate or what's on your computer screen. You can sense how much stimulation, input, or engagement you're up for and choose accordingly. For example, say you've set aside time for exercise and face a decision about what activity to pursue. As you notice your energy level and whether you wish to engage with others, you might decide on a game of tag with your kids, shooting hoops with a neighbor, or going for a solitary run or walk.

Here's another example: Say it's Thursday evening and you find that you have some unexpected free time available. Rather than making a habitual choice, such as turning on the TV or heading out to a local bar, you can pause, check in, and ask yourself "What's called for in this moment?" As you deeply pay attention to your body, thoughts, and emotions, you might find that you want to spend some time writing in your journal, call a loved one, catch up with friends on Facebook, do some yoga, or make a cup of tea and enjoy some time just being still.

Mindful Exploration: Feeling What's Called for in the Moment

Right now, take a few moments to consider what's called for in this moment. Deeply listen to your body, mind, and heart and see what arises. Be like a scientist, inquiring into your own experience.

As you reflected, what came up? What's called for now? And how did it feel to check in with yourself in this way?

____

____

Now go and do whatever seems to be called for now. Afterward, return and write about how it felt to engage in this activity, chosen from your own innate wisdom. What happened when you followed through on what arose? And how do you feel now?

____

____

____

Planning and Recording Your Practice

In this chapter, we focused on bringing more mindfulness to day-to-day life. We encourage you to continue doing formal practices daily and scheduling them in advance. As a reminder, the formal practices we've introduced thus far are the mindful check-in, mindful breathing, whole body awareness, the body scan, mindful floor yoga, mindful standing yoga, sitting meditation, narrow-gauge walking meditation, meditation on anxious emotions, insight dialogue, reconciliation meditation, and loving-kindness meditation. Over the next week, use the following practice log to record all of the practices you do—formal and informal—including those that arise spontaneously. You very well may discover that you're practicing more often than you think!

For each practice, briefly describe your experience. By this point, you may be feeling a new appreciation for the miracles—minor and not so minor—that tend to manifest when you show up for each moment of your life. Whatever the case may be, record your experiences in a spirit of opening to the unfolding moments of your life and learning to care for yourself, not judging or comparing. Let this log be a way of recognizing and acknowledging the ways you're actively participating in your own health and wellness, easing your anxiety, and coming home to more strength and peace. (For a downloadable version of this log, which will afford you as much space as you need to record all of your day-to-day experiences of mindfulness, visit http://www.newharbinger.com/29736; see the back of this book for information on how to access it.)

Formal and Informal Practice Log

Day and time: ______________________________

Your experience: ______________________________

____

Day and time: ______________________________

Your experience: ______________________________

____

Day and time: ______________________________

Your experience: ______________________________

____

Day and time: ______________________________

Your experience: ______________________________

____

Day and time: ______________________________

Your experience: ______________________________

____

Day and time: ______________________________

Your experience: ______________________________

____

Day and time: ______________________________

Your experience: ______________________________

____

Closing the Chapter

At this point in the book, you have a firm foundation in formal mindfulness practice. With this chapter, you've begun to extend the scope of your mindfulness to everyday activities and bringing awareness to what's called for in the moment. These approaches can go a long way toward alleviating feelings of anxiety. However, as a reminder, the path of mindfulness isn't like taking medication. It doesn't aim to make difficult feelings go away immediately and permanently. These feelings will quite naturally continue to arise from time to time, as they do for all people. However, with time and kindhearted, persistent practice, mindfulness can shift your perspective and change your symptoms, opening the door to a new experience of yourself. When your life lights up with mindfulness, transformation is possible. By making yourself receptive to it and beginning to appreciate the daily miracle of being alive, you open that door ever wider.

In the next chapter—the last chapter of this book—we'll give you a final few tools to help you navigate the mindful path as you journey forward. In the meanwhile, extend appreciation to yourself for your dedication and your journey thus far and consider the miracles that surround you. For a beautiful reflection on the common miracles we live with every day, take some time to absorb and reflect upon the following poem by Wisława Szymborska (2001, 119–120; reprinted with permission).

Miracle Fair

Commonplace miracle:
that so many commonplace miracles happen.

An ordinary miracle:
in the dead of night
the barking of invisible dogs.

One miracle out of many:
a small, airy cloud
yet it can block a large and heavy moon.

Several miracles in one:
an alder tree reflected in the water,
and that it's backwards left to right
and that it grows, there crown down
and never reaches the bottom,
even though the water is shallow.

An everyday miracle:
winds weak to moderate
turning gusty in storms...

A miracle (for what else could you call it):

today the sun rose three-fourteen
and will set at eight-o-one.

A miracle, just take a look around:
the world is everywhere.

Chapter 10

Continuing the Journey

As you begin to engage with this chapter, take a moment to reflect on your journey with this book. You've made a courageous choice to turn toward your experience, including anxiety, along the path to living more skillfully and with greater ease. Do you feel that you've come to understand yourself better as you've learned about anxiety and mindfulness? As you've explored and engaged with the practices throughout this book, have you made discoveries about how living mindfully can influence your relationship to yourself and your anxiety? As you've developed your capacity to tune in to bodily sensations, thoughts, and emotions in the moment, when you experience them, have you noticed that you're better able to tolerate the surge of experiences that arise in anxious moments? You may have discovered that your discipline and generosity have deepened with your commitment to formal and informal mindfulness practices. Hopefully you've begun to notice a kinder attitude toward yourself, as well.

With this final chapter, we want to support your growing ability to sense your connection and interconnection with yourself, others, the world, and even the universe around you. While you will inevitably experience anxiety in the future, as all people do, your ongoing mindfulness practice can serve as an anchor, helping you stay steady rather than being swept away by the tides of uncomfortable anxious feelings. In those moments, you no longer need to feel helpless, as you can now draw upon the strength and resilience that a formal meditation practice can bring. And through informal mindfulness practices, you can pause, ground yourself, and take refuge in the present moment, whatever you may be experiencing. This is a way of integrating mindfulness into the very fabric of your life and being. The choice to be mindful is always yours, and you can begin again at any moment.

Identifying Feeling Separate and Establishing Reconnection

In the past few chapters, we've offered many approaches that can enhance your sense of connection with others, such as mindful communication techniques and formal practices of reconciliation meditation and loving-kindness meditation. These approaches are immensely helpful in easing anxiety because feelings of being separate, disconnected, or, worse, unsupported, can all too easily snowball into anxiety, complete with all of the unpleasant symptoms anxiety can bring. A participant in an MBSR class once described this as feeling like she was in a bubble while the rest of the world was connected. She said she felt invisible, removed, and alone, and that it was gradually deepening her despair and a sense that she was different from everyone else and could never fit in. Perhaps you also have experienced this. The truth is, we all have moments when we feel isolated and painfully separate and long to experience our integral unity with life.

Mindfulness practice allows a different perspective and supports you in seeing what's actually happening. When you pause and recognize thoughts as just thoughts, emotions as just emotions, and sensations as bodily experiences, you develop a great sense of connection. While your present-moment experience may not be comfortable, you are in touch with the emerging moment, in touch with yourself, and quite possibly more in touch with other people. As your practice of mindfulness deepens, your sense of connection will gradually increase, easing your access to your deepest strengths and resources and to the whole of your life and the world.

Informal Practice: Reconnect

Here's an informal practice that you can do in the moment as soon as you recognize that you're feeling separate. There's no need to wait until you feel pain or a strong sense of disconnection; use it as soon as you have the sense that you'd like to feel more connected. You can do this practice in any position: lying down, sitting, or standing. One key way in which it differs from other practices in the book is that your eyes remain open and engaged with your surroundings.

First, deepen your awareness of your entire body. You might become aware of points of contact with the chair or surface beneath you, a sense of weight as you rest in the security of gravity, or a feeling of how you fully inhabit three dimensions through the length, width, and depth of your body. Pause here and invite a softening of any tension, perhaps in the belly, jaw, corners of the eyes, or hands. Allow your vision to expand, deliberately softening your gaze and widening the lens of your perception to take in your entire field of vision. Also connect with your breath and your heart, softening through your chest, being present, and actively bringing kindness to yourself.

Next, engage your visual field and body awareness together, opening your peripheral vision so you can be aware of your hands on your lap or more fully sense your entire body, perhaps your torso, thighs, or the width of your shoulders. Allow this sensory experience to extend to what you can see: light, colors, and shapes both in the foreground and the background, taking in the experience of being a part of the world. You might also expand to other senses, perhaps including smells and sounds as well. Allow yourself to become part of the fabric of the moment, seeing yourself in the wider field of your surroundings, hearing the sounds around you, feeling sensations in your body, and gently acknowledging any thoughts and feelings you find. Hold all of this spacious, open-eyed awareness.

Interconnectedness

Sensing yourself within the wider field of your surroundings is a practice that can broaden limitlessly as, throughout your day, you attend to the web of life that you're a part of and share with all living beings, all interconnected and interdependent. When you deeply reflect on the ripples of interconnection that pulse through your life, you can directly experience how you are never isolated. Everything in your life, from the food you eat to the furniture around you, connects you to the lives of others. We are all connected to our planet, nourished by its water and air. We are all connected to the sun, which supports all life on this planet. You exist within vibrating patterns of connection, which you will readily sense if you pause in any moment to feel your feet firmly planted on the earth, to receive the sun's warmth on your skin, to refresh yourself with a drink of water, and to sense how the flow of air as you breathe connects you with all of the life around you.

Being in nature and making time to experience and honor the natural elements of this world can provide a powerful reminder of the deep interconnection you have with this planet and all of its beings. Recognizing the forces of light and dark, gravity, weight, sunshine and moonlight, the cycles of seasons and weather—in short, the simple realities that unite us all—can be such a profound affirmation of everything you share with others and all of the ways in which you belong.

At times, it may also be helpful to recall the many ways in which you're connected with other people. For one, you're part of a network of millions of people around the globe who practice mindfulness. Whenever you take time to sit for meditation, practice the body scan, or engage in mindful movement, you join countless others who are also practicing at the very same time. While you may never meet these people in person, you enter into a global community of individuals making the choice to live with intention and become intimate with life in all of its vibrancy and interdependence.

Remembering your place in this community of practice, as well as your place in the human family and on this planet, you may choose to send kind wishes to yourself and others, and you may choose to open to receive the kind wishes of others. As mentioned, mindfulness is sometimes known as heartfulness, and this speaks to how the practice is both personally and interpersonally unifying. At any time, recalling this unity can break through feelings of disconnectedness or isolation, bringing a sense of interconnection that can suffuse you, like the sun emerging from a cover of clouds.

Formal Practice: Interconnection Meditation

This meditation will help strengthen your sense of interconnection. To allow you to fully experience this meditation without referring to the book, we recommend that you listen to the downloadable audio version, which is available at http://www.newharbinger.com/29736 (see the back of this book for instructions on how to access it). However, you can also simply read the text below. If you do this, read through the entire script first to familiarize yourself with the practice, then do the practice, referring back to the text as needed and pausing briefly after each paragraph. Set aside about twenty minutes for this practice. You can do it in a seated position, standing, or even lying down. Choose a position in which you can be comfortable and alert.

Begin by taking a few moments to check in with yourself and acknowledge how you're feeling physically, mentally, and emotionally. Whatever you find, allow it and let it all be.

Now gently shift awareness to breathing...being aware of breathing in and out, tuning in to one inhalation and one exhalation at a time. There's no need to manipulate your breath in any way; just breathe in and out normally and naturally. Try to focus on your breath wherever you feel it most distinctly. It could be at the tip of your nose, in your nostrils, or on your upper lip. You might feel it more prominently in your chest or belly or somewhere else. Wherever you feel your breath, let your awareness rest there...being mindful of breathing in and out.

Now begin to feel the connection of your body with the surface supporting you. Then feel how that surface is connected to the floor, which is connected to the building you're in, which is connected to the earth. Sense into this earth that holds you and allow yourself to be supported by it. Reflect on how this earth holds all beings, whether small or large, forsaking none. Reflect on how you're in a safe place and there's nothing more you need to do—nowhere you have to go, and no one you have to be. Just allow yourself to be held in the heart of the earth with kindness and ease.

Now let your awareness expand to sense the connection of the earth to the solar system and beyond, to the vast universe. In this way, we all are interconnected. Our bodies, the earth, and the stars—all are composed of the same matter. All are made up of the same basic particles, just joined in different and ever-changing ways. May you open to feeling at home within your body and mind with a true sense of belonging, connection, and interconnection.

Pause to feel into and relish the grace of this universe. Appreciate that you are an intrinsic part of it and can never be separated from it...feeling a sense of connection and interconnection as you are at home within your being. There's nothing you need to do and nothing to be pushed away...you are simply resting in the heart of this universe just as you are.

Now gradually return awareness to your breath and feel how your entire body breathes in and out, from head to toe to fingertip, unified, connected, and whole.

May all beings find the gateways into their hearts. May all beings feel at home within the world and universe.

Mindful Journaling

Right after your first practice of interconnection meditation, take a few moments to write about your experience. How did it go for you? How did you work with what came up within your body, thoughts, and emotions? And how are you feeling right now?

____

____

____

____

____

____

____

Formal Practice: Wide-Gauge Walking Meditation

Another way to practice interconnection is the wide-gauge walking meditation. It's called wide-gauge because it invites you to expand your awareness like a floodlight that sees and takes in the world in a larger way. This is a wonderful way to bring a sense of connection into your daily life: feeling your feet on the ground and making contact with the world around you.

To allow you to fully experience this meditation without referring to the book, we recommend that you listen to the downloadable audio version, which is available at http://www.newharbinger.com/29736. However, you can also simply read the text below. If you're reading the text, read through the entire script first to familiarize yourself with the practice, then do the practice, referring back to the text as needed and pausing briefly after each paragraph. Initially, take five to fifteen minutes for the practice. With time, you can extend the duration. If possible, practice this walking meditation outdoors.

> *Mindfully stand, coming to a balanced, upright posture. Feel into the way your feet are bearing your weight and pause for a moment, standing and knowing you are standing. Feel how your feet are making contact with the earth below and how you're connected to it. Then take a few moments to sense your head rising up toward the sky, making connection with the vast realms above.*
>
> *Now form an intention to take a step with your right foot and simply notice any bodily response to your intention. Next, lift your right foot, move it forward, and then place it back down. As you prepare to take a step with your left foot, feel your weight shift to your right foot, then lift*

your left foot, move it forward, and place it back down. Continue in this way, bringing awareness to the experience of walking one step at a time.

As you continue to walk, open awareness and attend to any senses that are calling out to you. You may notice sounds, aromas, or temperature. Allow the scope of your awareness to open to this wider range of perception…what your eyes see, what your ears hear, what your skin feels. Bring mindful awareness to a fuller experience of your body in movement, opening to the external environment and remaining aware of internal experiences.

Perhaps you might play with each footstep sending a blessing to you, the earth, and all beings. As you continue to walk, feel your connection to and place in this world and universe. May all beings be free.

As you're ready to finish this practice, take a moment to acknowledge yourself for devoting this time to yourself and mindfulness, nurturing your well-being and sense of ease and connection.

Mindful Journaling

Right after your first practice of wide-gauge walking meditation, take a few moments to write about your experience. How did it go for you? How did you work with what came up within your body, thoughts, and emotions? And how are you feeling right now?

____

____

____

____

____

____

____

Practice, Practice, Practice

There's an old story about a tourist in Manhattan asking a man with a violin case, "How do I get to Carnegie Hall?" Not knowing the man was famous violinist Jascha Heifetz, the tourist was surprised when he barked, "Practice!" As Heifetz understood through his own direct experience, you can't become an expert at something overnight. In any serious endeavor, the more you put into it, the more proficiency you'll gain.

The Foundation: Formal Practice

When a building's foundation is carefully crafted of strong materials and the structure is plumb, there's a stability that can support whatever comes next. The same is true of mindfulness practice, where steady consistency in formal practice provides a trustworthy support. At this point in the book, you've learned a number of formal practices, and you have access to recordings to support you in doing them. Now is a good time to check in and see which practices you're making time for. As a reminder, here are the practices you've learned:

- The mindful check-in
- Mindful breathing
- Whole body awareness
- The body scan
- Mindful floor yoga
- Mindful standing yoga
- Sitting meditation
- Narrow-gauge walking meditation
- Meditation on anxious emotions
- Insight dialogue
- Reconciliation meditation
- Loving-kindness meditation
- Interconnection meditation
- Wide-gauge walking meditation

For you, which are essential elements that you want to continue working with? Are you fitting those into your daily life in a regular way? If not, renew your commitment to yourself to do so, continuing to schedule your practices in advance. If follow-through is a problem, also consider posting reminders in places where you'll see them often.

Continuing to engage in formal mindfulness practices over the long term will support you in holding steady amidst sudden storms of anxiety, and will also improve your quality of life in general. With a regular, ongoing practice, the benefits can expand to include a greater appreciation for the life you've been given, a greater sense of sovereignty, and an enhanced ability to make wise choices, including choices about how you live. In this sense, mindfulness is a lifelong way of being.

Practice Pointers

Like any skill, your mindfulness practice will be strengthened and refined by daily repetition. Commitment matters, and even reminders to practice bear repetition! Below, we offer some pointers (and some reminders) to support you in your daily practice and your ongoing quest to bring more mindfulness to your day-to-day life. Infusing your practice with these qualities can enhance and support your entire being by engendering self-regard, confidence, and stability. And there's no reason to limit your focus on these attributes to formal practice. As you embrace mindfulness as a way of life, these qualities can support a new perspective, one in which you bring the depth of your inner resources to bear on the fullness of your experience.

Resolve. Choosing to maintain a regular practice takes resolve in bringing discipline and courage to beginning again and again. You can refresh your resolve each day, perhaps by stating an intention to do so when you arise. Manifest your resolution by bringing firmness to your moment-to-moment practice and returning to the present whenever you discover that you've been caught in streams of fantasy. Bringing kindness to that process of returning to the moment is also an expression of resolve. And, of course, choosing to live mindfully is a way of extending your resolve to encompass your entire life.

Prioritization. Choosing to make time to practice formal meditation each day prioritizes a way of life that will build your resilience over time. It also supports your informal practice of remembering to be awake to the unfolding moments of your everyday life. Reflecting on the benefits you experience may help you prioritize your practice. As a man who was diagnosed with an anxiety disorder explained it, once he learned the power of mindfulness to help him live with more ease, he had no difficulty prioritizing daily practice. He said, "Now I can take a shower and truly enjoy the experience of warmth and the water flowing over my body. In the past, I would have been absorbed in worries about what might happen in the future. Each moment of my life is so much fuller now."

Patience. A seed doesn't sprout and blossom overnight. Think of your practice of mindfulness as a garden you're planting and imagine that you're preparing the soil with your intention to respond more gracefully to everything that happens. In this well-tilled soil, you can plant the seeds of the strength to be as you are, where you are, and fertilize them with curiosity and kindness. You're growing a new way of living, and this takes time and patience. Although it's all too human to want life to be different, meeting any desires for particular results or rapid changes with patience will allow you to rest more easily with things as they are.

Acknowledgment and recognition. Encouragement facilitates growth, so it's important to extend acknowledgment and recognition to yourself. As you continue to develop your daily mindfulness practice, take time to stop and acknowledge the values you're choosing to live by. Give yourself credit for taking such an active role in your own health and well-being. This is no small choice, so pause often and honor the power of choosing to enhance the quality of your life. Recognize yourself for being willing to make a personal investment in each new day.

Kindness. Practicing kindness creates a strong foundation from which you can turn toward your life with stability and ease. Affectionate attentiveness waters the seeds of loving your life as it is and living with greater wisdom. Kind attention to yourself is especially important when you feel anxious or vulnerable. Often, these are exactly the times when old patterns of judgment and criticism creep in. The more you can offer yourself compassion, the more courage you'll have to continue on the path of mindfulness, living in deep connection with your natural resources of strength and flexibility.

Also bear in mind that you always have four ways of practice available to you: sitting, standing, lying down, or while in motion. The beauty of this is that in any moment of your day, in whatever position you may be in, you have the opportunity to come into the present moment by shifting awareness to your bodily sensations, thoughts, and emotions. You might do this for an extended period of time or for just a few moments. In either case, you're gathering your energy and enhancing your sense of vitality. This is true whether you're anxious or calm, happy or sad, tired or energized, bored or filled with wonder. There's no need to wait to fully inhabit your life. It's yours to claim, and no one can do this but you.

Exercise: Assessing Your Anxiety Level

As this book comes to an end, take some time to once again complete this informal anxiety assessment, as you did when you began reading this book. As a reminder, this is a two-step process:

1. Using the form below, list up to ten situations that you currently feel anxious about. Feel free to list everyday experiences of anxiety or really zero in on specific things. Ideally, you'd once again list at least a few of the same the items as you did originally so you can compare your scores and see whether your anxiety levels have changed.
2. Rate how you feel about each situation on a scale of 1 to 10, with 1 being not very anxious and 10 being extremely anxious.

One important note: If you continue to assign high ratings (8 to 10) to most of the situations listed, we highly recommend that you seek support from a health care or mental health professional.

Rating	Situation
______	____
______	____
______	____
______	____
______	____

______ ____

______ ____

______ ____

______ ____

MINDFUL PAUSE

Take a few moments to reflect upon your journey with this book and what you've discovered and learned along the way. Acknowledge and appreciate yourself for the work you've done to nurture your well being. You've planted seeds that will grow and blossom into more peace and ease into your life.

Closing the Book

We hope you'll choose to establish a regular, ongoing practice, as this will continue to strengthen your ability to turn toward whatever is present, moment to moment. We encourage you to make a concerted effort to experiment with a period of dedicated practice, engaging in formal meditation regularly and remembering to weave mindfulness into routine daily activities, which so often go unnoticed. Consider choosing to engage in everything you've learned, fully and on a daily basis, for a certain period of time—perhaps two months—suspending judgment until that time has ended. Commit to specific times and places to practice, and put them on your calendar. Also consider continuing to keep a record of your practice, perhaps using the practice log at the end of chapter 9. Remember, building new habits takes practice. See what you discover during this time, and when it comes to an end, check in with yourself regarding the quality of your day-to-day life. See for yourself if you notice any increase in your sense of calm, equanimity, flexibility, compassion, or strength.

After this chapter you'll find a resources section, filled with recommended readings and other information to support you in maintaining your mindfulness practice as a way of life. It can be very strengthening to gather with like-minded people who are also making the powerful choice to intervene directly in the quality of their lives by cultivating greater freedom and compassion through the practice of mindfulness, so we've also included information on MBSR programs, local meditation groups, and retreat centers. Consider gifting yourself with the powerful experience of practicing with others. In such a unique environment, the feeling of community and support is palpable. Many people find that practicing with others on a weekly or monthly basis fuels their individual practice. This is one of the most profound ways of being connected: entering into the collective energy of a community dedicated to mindful awareness.

Our wish is for you to live with greater ease, happiness, and understanding. Through your deepening practice, may you experience the truth of your own integrity and wholeness, find increasing freedom from anxiety, and discover the innate brilliance that dwells within you *as* you. May you also feel, at a very deep level, your interconnection with others, manifested even here and now, as you read our wishes for your well-being. As this chapter, and this book, comes to a close, please read and reflect upon this poem by Dan Shanahan (2003; printed with permission). It speaks beautifully to the web of interconnection that always surrounds and holds you.

Lotus Seed Poem 18

Have you seen
How trees
Use their shadows
To embrace other trees?
Even now someone or something
From somewhere
Is loving us with the deep silence of the forest.

Resources

Online Resources

Mindfulness-Based Stress Reduction Programs

Mindfulness-based stress reduction programs abound throughout the United States and internationally. Here are some resources that can help you track down local and online offerings:

- To find a local MBSR class, you can check with hospitals and medical centers in your area, or try typing your geographic area followed by "MBSR" into a search engine.
- Online mindfulness classes: http://www.emindful.com and http://www.soundstrue.com/mbsr

General Mindfulness Resources and Information on Mindfulness Research

For more information on mindfulness, research findings, and helpful resources, visit the following websites:

- The Center for Mindfulness at the University of Massachusetts Medical School: http://www.umassmed.edu/cfm (includes a link to an order form for MBSR CDs and DVDs)
- Mindfulness Research Monthly: http://www.mindfulexperience.org

- Mind and Life Institute: http://www.mindandlife.org
- Mindful Awareness Research Center: http://www.marc.ucla.edu
- Mindsight Institute: https://www.mindsightinstitute.com
- MBSR blog and weekly inspirational emails: http://www.soundstrue.com/mbsr

Mindfulness Meditation Centers and Weekly Sitting Groups

To find mindfulness meditation centers and weekly sitting groups in the United States, consult the following websites, which also provide contact information for international insight meditation centers:

- For the West Coast: http://www.spiritrock.org
- For the East Coast: http://www.dharma.org

Internet Resources for Anxiety

The following websites offer more information on anxiety:

- Anxiety Disorders Association of America: http://www.adaa.org
- The Anxiety Panic Internet Resource: http://www.algy.com/anxiety
- International OCD Foundation: http://www.ocfoundation.org

Meditation Timers

You can download a number of free meditation timers online, including from the Insight Meditation Center, at http://www.insightmeditationcenter.org/meditation-timers.

Mindfulness Meditation Audio CDs and DVDs by Bob Stahl

To purchase or listen to samples from the following CDs, visit http://www.mindfulnessprograms.com and click on the link to Mindfulness CDs and DVDs. You can also purchase all except the last four at http://www.amazon.com.

- *Opening to Change, Forgiveness, and Lovingkindness*
- *Working with Chronic Pain*
- *Working with Neck and Shoulder Pain*
- *Working with Back Pain*
- *Working with Insomnia and Sleep Challenges*
- *Working with Anxiety, Fear, and Panic*
- *Working with High Blood Pressure*
- *Working with Heart Disease*
- *Working with Headaches and Migraines*
- *Working with Asthma, COPD, and Respiratory Challenges*
- *Body Scan and Sitting Meditation*
- *Lying and Standing Yoga*
- *Impermanence and Lovingkindness Meditation*
- *Mindful Qigong and Lovingkindness Meditation*

Recommended Reading

For a list of recommended reading, including poetry and other inspirational readings, texts on mindfulness and anxiety, and other books by Bob Stahl, visit http://www.newharbinger.com/29736 (see the back of this book for instructions on how to access the list).

References

Center for Mindfulness in Medicine, Health Care, and Society, University of Massachusetts Medical School. 2014. "Research: Major Research Studies and Findings." http://www.umassmed.edu/Content.aspx?id=42426. Accessed March 9, 2014.

Davidson, R. J., J. Kabat-Zinn, J. Schumacher, M. Rosenkranz, D. Muller, S. F. Santorelli, F. Urbanowski, A. Harrington, K. Bonus, and J. F. Sheridan. 2003. "Alterations in Brain and Immune Function Produced by Mindfulness Meditation." *Psychosomatic Medicine* 65(4):564–570.

Descartes, R. 1999. *Discourse on Method and Related Writings*. London: Penguin Books.

Faulds, D. 2002. *Go In and In: Poems from the Heart of Yoga*. Greenville, VA: Danna Faulds.

———. 2009. Limitless: New Poems and Other Writings. Greenville, VA: Danna Faulds.

Golden, P., and J. Gross. 2010. "Effects of Mindfulness-Based Stress Reduction (MBSR) on Emotion Regulation in Social Anxiety Disorder." *Emotion* 10(1):83–91.

Goyal, M., S. Singh, E. M. S. Sibinga, N. F. Gould, A. Rowland-Seymour, R. Sharma … J. A. Haythornthwaite. 2014. "Meditation Programs for Psychological Stress and Well-Being: A Systematic review and Meta-Analysis." *Journal of the American Medical Association Internal Medicine* 174(3):357–368.

Greenberg, P. E., T. Sisitsky, R. C. Kessler, S. N. Finkelstein, E. R. Berndt, J. R. Davidson, J. C. Ballenger, and A. J. Fyer. 1999. "The Economic Burden of Anxiety Disorders in the 1990s." *Journal of Clinical Psychiatry* 60(7):427–435.

Hofmann, S. G., A. T. Sawyer, A. A. Witt, and D. Oh. 2010. "The Effect of Mindfulness-Based Therapy on Anxiety and Depression: A Meta-Analytic Review." *Journal of Consulting and Clinical Psychology* 78(2):169–183.

Hölzel, B. K., J. Carmody, K. C. Evans, E. A. Hoge, J. A. Dusek, L. Morgan, R. K. Pitman, and S. W. Lazar. 2010. "Stress Reduction Correlates with Structural Changes in the Amygdala." *Social Cognitive and Affective Neuroscience* 5(1):11–17.

Johnson, W. 2000. *Aligned, Relaxed, Resilient: The Physical Foundations of Mindfulness.* Boston, MA: Shambhala.

Kabat-Zinn, J. 2007. *Arriving at Your Own Door: 108 Lessons in Mindfulness.* New York: Hyperion.

Kabir. 2004. *Kabir: Ecstatic Poems,* translated by R. Bly. Boston: Beacon.

Kramer, G. 2007. *Insight Dialogue: The Interpersonal Path to Freedom.* Boston: Shambhala.

Lazarus, R. S., and S. Folkman. 1984. *Stress, Appraisal, and Coping.* New York: Springer.

Levey, J., and M. Levey. 2009. *Luminous Mind: Meditation and Mind Fitness.* San Francisco: Red Wheel.

Miller, J., K. Fletcher, and J. Kabat-Zinn. 1995. "Three-Year Follow-Up and Clinical Implications of a Mindfulness Meditation–Based Stress Reduction Intervention in the Treatment of Anxiety Disorders." *General Hospital Psychiatry* 17(3):192–200.

Milton, J. 2005. *Paradise Lost.* Indianapolis, IN: Hackett Publishing.

National Institute of Mental Health. 2008. "The Numbers Count: Mental Disorders in America." http://www.nimh.nih.gov/health/publications/the-numbers-count-mental-disorders-in-america/index.shtml#Intro. Accessed March 17, 2014.

Nhat Hanh, Thich. 1992. *Touching Peace: Practicing the Art of Mindful Living.* Berkeley, CA: Parallax Press.

Shanahan, D. 2003. *The Lotus Seed Poems.* Audio CD of poems by Dan Shanahan accompanied on guitar by Nicolas Despo.

Stafford, W. 1998. *The Way It Is: New and Selected Poems.* St. Paul, MN: Graywolf Press.

Szymborska, W. 2001. *Miracle Fair: Selected Poems of Wisława Szymborska.* New York: W. W. Norton.

Thera, N. (translator). 2004. *The Dhammapada.* Whitefish, MT: Kessinger Publications.

Welwood, J. P. 1998. *Poems for the Path.* Mill Valley, CA: Jennifer Paine Welwood.

Whyte, D. 1997. *House of Belonging.* Langley, WA: Many Rivers Company.

Williams, M. 1997. *The Ways We Touch.* Chicago: University of Illinois Press.

Bob Stahl, PhD, founded and directs mindfulness-based stress reduction (MBSR) programs at Dominican Hospital and El Camino Hospital. Stahl also serves as a senior teacher for Oasis Institute for Mindfulness-Based Professional Education and Training at the Center for Mindfulness in Medicine, Health Care, and Society at the University of Massachusetts Medical School. Stahl is a coauthor of *A Mindfulness-Based Stress Reduction Workbook*, *Living With Your Heart Wide Open*, and *Calming the Rush of Panic*. He is the guiding teacher at Insight Santa Cruz and visiting teacher at Spirit Rock Meditation Center and Insight Meditation Society.

Florence Meleo-Meyer, MS, MA, is director of Oasis Institute for Mindfulness-Based Professional Education and Training at the Center for Mindfulness in Medicine, Health Care, and Society at the University of Massachusetts Medical School. Meleo-Meyer is a leading international teacher who has helped develop and offer professional trainings for MBSR teachers for over eighteen years. In addition to teaching in the mindfulness-based stress reduction (MBSR) program, she has offered mindfulness programs to educators, physicians, psychologists, and young adults.

Lynn Koerbel, MPH, is associate director of Oasis Institute for Mindfulness-Based Professional Education and Training at the Center for Mindfulness in Medicine, Health Care, and Society at the University of Massachusetts Medical School. Koerbel cofounded Present Moment Mindfulness in Western Massachusetts, a community-based organization offering MBSR classes and mindfulness-based applications in the fields of education, business, and health. Prior to teaching MBSR, she worked in the field of integrative bodywork for almost twenty-five years, with a focus on healing from trauma and the integration of the body in healing.

Foreword writer **Saki Santorelli, EdD, MA**, is executive director of the Center for Mindfulness in Medicine, Health Care, and Society at the University of Massachusetts Medical School and author of *Heal Thy Self*.

FROM OUR PUBLISHER—

As the publisher at New Harbinger and a clinical psychologist since 1978, I know that emotional problems are best helped with evidence-based therapies. These are the treatments derived from scientific research (randomized controlled trials) that show what works. Whether these treatments are delivered by trained clinicians or found in a self-help book, they are designed to provide you with proven strategies to overcome your problem.

Therapies that aren't evidence-based—whether offered by clinicians or in books—are much less likely to help. In fact, therapies that aren't guided by science may not help you at all. That's why this New Harbinger book is based on scientific evidence that the treatment can relieve emotional pain.

This is important: if this book isn't enough, and you need the help of a skilled therapist, use the following resources to find a clinician trained in the evidence-based protocols appropriate for your problem. And if you need more support—a community that understands what you're going through and can show you ways to cope—resources for that are provided below, as well.

Real help is available for the problems you have been struggling with. The skills you can learn from evidence-based therapies will change your life.

Matthew McKay, PhD
Publisher, New Harbinger Publications

If you need a therapist, the following organization can help you find a therapist trained in cognitive behavioral therapy (CBT).

The Association for Behavioral & Cognitive Therapies (ABCT) Find-a-Therapist service offers a list of therapists schooled in CBT techniques. Therapists listed are licensed professionals who have met the membership requirements of ABCT and who have chosen to appear in the directory.

Please visit www.abct.org and click on *Find a Therapist*.

For additional support for patients, family, and friends, please contact the following:

Anxiety and Depression Association of American (ADAA)
please visit www.adaa.org

National Alliance on Mental Illness (NAMI)
please visit www.nami.org

National Suicide Prevention Lifeline
Call 24 hours a day 1-800-273-TALK (8255) or visit www.suicidepreventionlifeline.org